COOK WITH LOVE

COOK WITH LOVE

the PETE EVANS COLLECTION

MURDOCH BOOKS

contents

My greatest hits

Selecting the recipes to include here from the thousands I've written was tough but also pretty cool; re-reading the recipes from my previous books and looking through the beautiful pictures was like taking a walk down memory lane. It gave me a chance to reflect on my twenty-plus-years as a chef and appreciate the incredible journey that cooking has taken me on, the inspirational people it has introduced me to, and the adventures I've had because of it.

When I started my cooking career I was young, hungry for respect and eager to prove that I could run my own kitchens. I worked hard and had the good fortune to find myself executive chef for the successful restaurant group Hugos. I designed menus for the restaurants, cooked elegant food at high-profile events, and got to travel and learn more about food from other countries. Eventually, as my children got a bit older, I began spending less time in commercial kitchens and more time cooking at home for my family and friends. Some of the fancy, technical dishes gave way to simpler, family-style food. I focused on cooking the best produce as possible simply, so the flavours could speak for themselves. Cooking has become much more about health and nutrition, and that in itself has taken me on another journey.

This is reflected throughout the books I've had published. I've had so much fun making them with the publishers, photographers, editors and stylists I've worked with over the years. *Fish* was a celebration of the variety and versatility of Aussie and Kiwi seafood. *My Grill* was all about using flames, whether from a campfire or a barbecue, to create really memorable meals. *My Table* and *My Party* gave me a chance to share a lot of the things I had learned about entertaining, like how to throw a great themed party or how to make incredible canapés. In *My Kitchen* I brought things back to the home, and focused on family-friendly meals. And then *Pizza*, the most recent of my books, was my take on the pizza recipes I'd been collecting and creating over my many years in the restaurant business.

And so I like to think of this book as my 'greatest hits', a snapshot of my years in the kitchen to date. Each recipe is here for a reason: either because I still cook it all the time, a special person shared it with me, or someone once told me it's the best thing they've ever tasted. I hope you will enjoy the range of styles, techniques and ingredients to choose from all brought together in one cookbook.

Once you know how to cook, you can adapt your style to any situation, whether it's lunch for your mum or dinner over a campfire. That's what this book is all about. There is a time and a place for everything, fancy and simple. I've always loved seafood, so there's a chapter dedicated to seafood, including everything from an elegant tuna tartare to a whole curried side of salmon. There are delicate little canapés for entertaining as well as serious dishes for those nights when you want to make a real impression in 'Showing Off'. And, because most of us are looking for great things

to cook in our day-to-day lives, there are also plenty of family-friendly recipes such as my slow-roasted pork or pot-roasted chicken that I guarantee will have people, young and old, coming back for seconds (maybe even thirds).

I've always said that if even one of my recipes becomes a part of someone's cooking repertoire, I'm a happy man. That's as true now as it's always been. I hope you enjoy.

Cook with love and laughter,

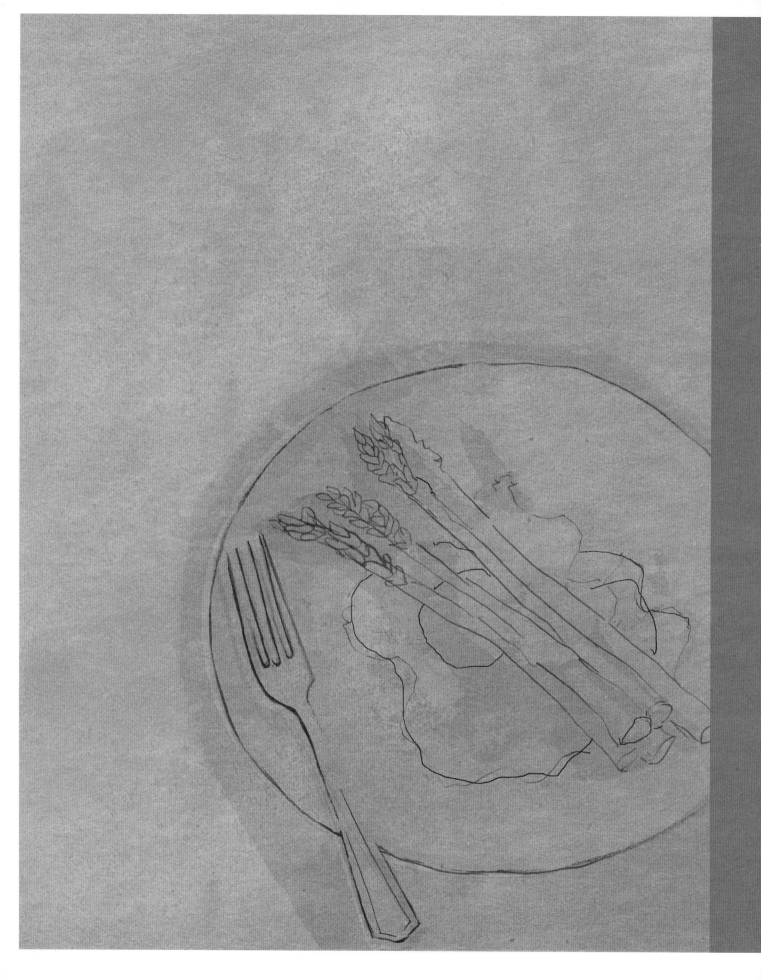

start the day

A lot of health experts will say that breakfast is the most important meal of the day, and I couldn't agree more. I can't imagine getting through a morning without some good food in my system — I'd be a zombie! What I eat for breakfast these days depends on what the weather is like, how much time I've got, and who I'm cooking for. The bircher muesli on page 2 is perfect for a weekday breakfast when time is short, whereas something like the huevos rancheros on page 17 is a beautiful thing to cook on a weekend away. It's spicy, hearty and an exciting change from the usual toast and cereal routine. If you tend to skip breakfast, I hope this chapter convinces you that you're seriously missing out.

I don't know about you, but I love to start the day with something good in my system. For me, breakfast is the time to do the right thing by my body and there are few things better for you than Bircher muesli. It was named for the Swiss doctor, Maximilian Bircher-Benner, who created it back in the early 1900s. The recipe has stood the test of time, and the thing I love most about it is that you can vary the ingredients to suit your own tastes and the seasonality of the fruit. If you are following a gluten-free diet, you can make a version of this using mixed nuts and seeds and some coconut flakes in place of the oats.

bircher muesli

SERVES 4

Combine the oats, milk, apple juice and lemon juice in a large bowl. Cover with plastic wrap and refrigerate overnight.

Mix the grated apple through the oat mixture, then divide among four bowls. Add the banana, berries, walnuts and dried apricots. Drizzle with the honey and yoghurt and top with mint leaves.

200 g (7 oz/2 cups) rolled (porridge) oats
250 ml (9 fl oz/1 cup) milk
250 ml (9 fl oz/1 cup) apple juice
juice of 1 lemon
2 apples, coarsely grated
1 banana, chopped
125 g (4½ oz/1 cup) mixed berries (blackberries, blueberries, strawberries, raspberries)
3 tablespoons chopped walnuts
4 dried apricots or dried figs
3 tablespoons honey
125 g (4½ oz/½ cup) plain yoghurt
8 mint leaves

This very impressive breakfast looks fantastic, but takes very little time to put together. It also makes a great dinner if you've invited a vegetarian over and find yourself in a panic about what to cook them. The great thing about this dish is that when you break open the poached egg, the yolk spills out and mingles with the nut brown butter sauce. Fresh shavings of the best parmesan or truffled pecorino are a must for this, and the addition of some truffle oil or shaved truffle will help lift it to another dimension.

asparagus with poached egg, nut brown butter & truffled pecorino

SERVES 4

2 bunches of asparagus
4 free-range eggs
1 teaspoon white wine vinegar
2 tablespoons butter
1 teaspoon crushed garlic
2 teaspoons chopped parsley
a squeeze of lemon juice
crumbled truffled pecorino cheese
   or parmesan shavings (optional)

Boil the asparagus in salted water until just tender, then drain. Poach the eggs in just simmering water with the white wine vinegar added. Heat the butter in a frying pan until it starts to turn brown. Add the garlic, parsley, asparagus, lemon juice and some salt and pepper.

Arrange the asparagus on plates and top with the poached eggs. Drizzle some of the sauce around the plates and over the eggs, then top with the pecorino or parmesan shavings.

I love to use salmon caviar on everything from salads to raw seafood because it's full of omega-3s and adds a real textural burst of excitement to any dish. My favourite way to use it is simply with fresh free-range eggs, either boiled, as here, or poached. I was fortunate enough to witness the milking of salmon a few years ago. There is a two-week period each year when they are ready to spawn and it was amazing to watch. The salmon are placed in a clove bath to anaesthetise them, then quickly taken out of the water and gently milked to remove the eggs. Then they're popped back into the water, unharmed. The caviar is then blast frozen and defrosted throughout the year as the market demands.

soft-boiled eggs with salmon caviar

SERVES 4

Place the eggs in a saucepan of lightly salted water and bring to the boil. Reduce the heat and simmer for 3–4 minutes, then lift out.

Cut the tops off the eggs and season lightly with salt and pepper. Spoon a teaspoon of salmon roe into each egg. Serve with toasted brioche or sourdough soldiers.

8 free-range eggs
4 teaspoons salmon roe (or other caviar you like)
8 slices of brioche or sourdough, toasted

This recipe is very simple: some eggs, bread and maple syrup or honey for the batter, fried on the barbecue or in a pan until golden and then slathered with your favourite toppings. This one features honey, ricotta and figs, which is actually a great combination on its own but even better when teamed with the golden French toast. Try experimenting with different types of bread. I've recently been buying a sprouted seed bread that's wheat and gluten-free and perfect for French toast.

french toast with figs

SERVES 4

6 free-range eggs
2 tablespoons maple syrup or honey
8 slices of bread (whatever type you like)
8 fresh figs, cut or torn in half
90 g (3¼ oz/¼ cup) organic honey, warmed
icing (confectioners') sugar, to dust (optional)
8 tablespoons ricotta cheese

Preheat the barbecue hotplate or frying pan to medium. Beat the eggs with the maple syrup or honey and a pinch of sea salt. Soak each piece of bread in the egg mix for about 10 seconds so that the bread goes a bit soggy.

Drain off the excess egg from the bread and place onto the lightly greased barbecue hotplate or pan. Cook for 2–3 minutes until golden on one side, then flip over and cook until golden on the other side.

Cook the figs, cut-side down, for 1–2 minutes or until golden and then place onto a platter with the French toast. Drizzle with the honey and dust with icing sugar. Serve with ricotta cheese.

I love chorizo sausages. These Spanish pork sausages are flavoured with paprika and a staple in my fridge. They are so versatile — I use them in everything from rice and pasta dishes, with seafood, in stews and, my favourite, with eggs for breakfast. This is a simple recipe that can be cooked in a pan or on the barbecue with a minimum of fuss and is a great way to start the day — especially on holidays.

eggs with chorizo

SERVES 4

Preheat the barbecue grill or oven grill to high. Cook the capsicum on the grill, turning occasionally, for 15–20 minutes or until the skin turns black. Remove from the barbecue and let cool. Wipe away the skin leaving the capsicum flesh. Cut in half, remove the seeds and stalk and cut into strips.

Meanwhile, cook the tomatoes for a few minutes until tender, then cut into chunky pieces.

Place the chorizo slices on the barbecue hotplate or pan, cook until golden on each side then combine in a bowl with the capsicum, tomato, parsley and salt and pepper.

Place the chorizo and capsicum mix in a cast-iron frying pan. Make some holes in the mix to crack the eggs into. Add the eggs, then sprinkle with paprika and manchego cheese. Cover and cook over medium heat for about 5 minutes, or until the egg whites are cooked and the yolks are runny. This is delicious served on toasted sourdough bread.

1 red capsicum (pepper)
4 tomatoes, halved
1 chorizo sausage, cut into slices
1 small handful of torn flat-leaf (Italian) parsley
8 free-range eggs
pinch of smoked paprika
100 g (3½ oz/1 cup) cup grated manchego cheese

This is without a doubt one of the best-ever breakfast recipes for eggs and seafood. Hollandaise sounds scary but it is really quite simple to make — you just need to remember that the water in the pot should be barely simmering, so that you don't overheat the yolks and scramble them, and you must add the butter slowly to prevent the sauce separating. It is also important to use the sauce within about half an hour of making it.

If you're feeling really extravagant, try whisking some sea urchin roe into the hollandaise. This sauce is glorious on just about any grilled or poached seafood.

eggs benedict with smoked salmon

SERVES 4

HOLLANDAISE SAUCE
2 free-range egg yolks
1–2 tablespoons tarragon or white
    wine vinegar
125 ml (4 fl oz/½ cup) melted butter
1 teaspoon chopped chives
a wedge of lemon (optional)

a couple of drops of vinegar for
    poaching the eggs
8 free-range eggs
4 English muffins
butter for the muffins
200 g (7 oz) baby English spinach
    leaves
8 slices smoked salmon
salmon roe or caviar (if you're feeling
    indulgent)

To make the hollandaise sauce, half-fill a saucepan with water and bring to the boil. Turn off the heat. Put the egg yolks and vinegar in a stainless steel mixing bowl and put that over the saucepan. Start whisking fast until when you lift up your whisk the ribbons that run off it into the bowl 'sit' on top of the mixture for about 3 seconds (this is the ribbon stage). Slowly add the melted butter in a thin stream, still whisking fast. Season with some salt and white pepper, chives and a touch of lemon juice if you like.

Bring about 1 litre (35 fl oz/4 cups) of water to the boil in a large wide pan and add a few drops of vinegar to the water (this helps the eggs hold their shape when you poach them). You might find it easier to bring two pans of water to the boil and cook 4 eggs in each.

When the water comes to the bowl, crack the eggs into a bowl first (so they are all ready to cook at exactly the same moment), slide them into the water and turn the water temperature down to a simmer. Cook to your own taste (I like my eggs runny, so 3–4 minutes). Toast and butter your muffins while the eggs are cooking.

Meanwhile, blanch the spinach in boiling salted water and then drain, or alternatively heat a little olive oil in a pan and quickly cook the spinach leaves, then drain and season.

Lay smoked salmon over the muffins, spoon spinach onto the salmon, pop your eggs on top of the spinach, ladle some of your hollandaise over the eggs and finish with some salmon roe or caviar.

If you look at breakfasts from around the world, hardly any include milk, cereal or bread. In Asia, breakfast is more likely to be a broth that is served with rice or noodles and sometimes some protein. I think this is a wonderful way to start the day. Give this congee a try — you can speed up the process by using some leftover rice from the night before and, if you're like me, you'll have some small containers of frozen chicken stock waiting in the freezer to pull out for a dish such as this.

lap cheong & egg congee, my way

SERVES 4

Place the rice, stock and ginger in a large saucepan and bring to the boil. Reduce to a simmer and cook for 30 minutes, or until the rice starts to soften and break down.

Meanwhile, heat a frying pan with a little oil and fry the sausage or bacon until just starting to become crisp, then remove and reserve.

When the rice is lovely and soupy, add the sausage, coriander, spring onion, chilli and soy sauce. Season with white pepper and a pinch of sea salt. Return to the boil. Divide among four bowls and crack an egg into the centre of each one. Allow to stand for 3–5 minutes so the heat of the congee cooks the eggs. Sprinkle with sesame seeds and drizzle with sesame oil, if you like.

NOTE: Lap cheong are dried Chinese pork sausages available vacuum-packed at select supermarkets and Asian food stores.

740 g (1 lb 10 oz/4 cups) cooked long-grain white rice
2.5 litres (10 cups) chicken stock
65 g (2¼ oz/⅓ cup) thinly sliced fresh ginger
olive oil
4 Chinese sausages (lap cheong), sliced, or 2 slices of bacon, sliced (see Note)
1 handful of roughly chopped coriander (cilantro)
50 g (1¾ oz/¾ cup) thinly sliced spring onion (scallion), white and green part
4 bird's eye chillies, thinly sliced
80 ml (2½ fl oz/⅓ cup) soy sauce
ground white pepper
4 free-range eggs
toasted sesame seeds, for garnish
sesame oil, for garnish (optional)

This is a dish I created about twenty years ago with Leela, one of the many talented chefs I've worked with over the years. Leela was from the United States and we worked the breakfast shift together (my favourite part of the week – organised chaos). She suggested we put huevos rancheros on the menu and I said 'qué?' She patiently explained that it's a tremendously famous Mexican breakfast dish (meaning 'ranchers' eggs') and over the next week or two we came up with the dish as it stands today. This went on to become our biggest breakfast-time seller in Bondi, and I have yet to meet someone who doesn't love it. Thanks Leela; you're a champion!

huevos rancheros

SERVES 4

2 tablespoons olive oil
4 corn tortillas or enchilada tortillas
4 free-range eggs
8 tablespoons refried beans or Mexican beans
8 tablespoons Mexican salsa (your favourite brand)
1 tablespoon chopped coriander (cilantro) leaves
60 g (2 oz/½ cup) grated cheddar cheese
1 avocado, peeled and sliced
4 tablespoons sour cream
4 coriander (cilantro) sprigs
1 lime, cut into quarters
12 jalapeño peppers (if you like)
Green Tabasco sauce (optional)

Preheat your grill or oven. Heat the oil in a frying pan and fry the tortillas on both sides until just starting to brown, then place on a baking tray.

Fry your eggs until they are just cooked but the yolks are still soft.

Spread 2 tablespoons of beans over each tortilla. Top with 2 tablespoons of salsa, place an egg on top of the salsa and season with sea salt and pepper. Sprinkle with the coriander and cheese.

Grill or bake in the oven just until the cheese has melted, then put on plates. Top each serving with avocado slices and a spoonful of sour cream. Garnish with coriander sprigs, and serve with lime wedges and jalapeño peppers. If you want this extra hot, splash on a bit of green Tabasco sauce before serving.

The jury is out (well, mine is anyway!) on what tastes better: brown or rainbow trout. Rainbow trout is much easier to find in the marketplace, but I think a smoked, freshly-caught brown trout is a magical thing. You could also use smoked salmon, crabmeat or sea urchin. When I'm trout fishing in the mountains I like to have a hearty breakfast and the unique combination of tarragon, horseradish and smoked trout is like cheese and crackers — it just works. Keep in mind that horseradish is a pretty punchy ingredient, so start lightly and add more to taste. If you can't get smoked trout, try smoked salmon, crabmeat or sea urchin.

scrambled eggs with smoked trout, tarragon & horseradish

SERVES 4

Whisk the eggs and cream together and season with a pinch of sea salt and pepper. Heat the butter and olive oil in a non-stick frying pan over medium heat until hot, but not coloured. Pour in the eggs and cook, stirring with a wooden spoon until they are just starting to firm up. Add the trout and tarragon and serve immediately on toast, topped with grated horseradish, caviar and a lemon wedge.

8 free-range eggs
250 ml (9 fl oz/1 cup) pouring cream
40 g (1½ oz) butter
2 tablespoons extra virgin olive oil
1½ cups flaked smoked trout flesh (you will need 1–2 trout for this amount)
30 tarragon leaves, torn
4 pieces of toast
grated horseradish, to taste
4 tablespoons caviar (salmon or sturgeon)
lemon wedges, to serve

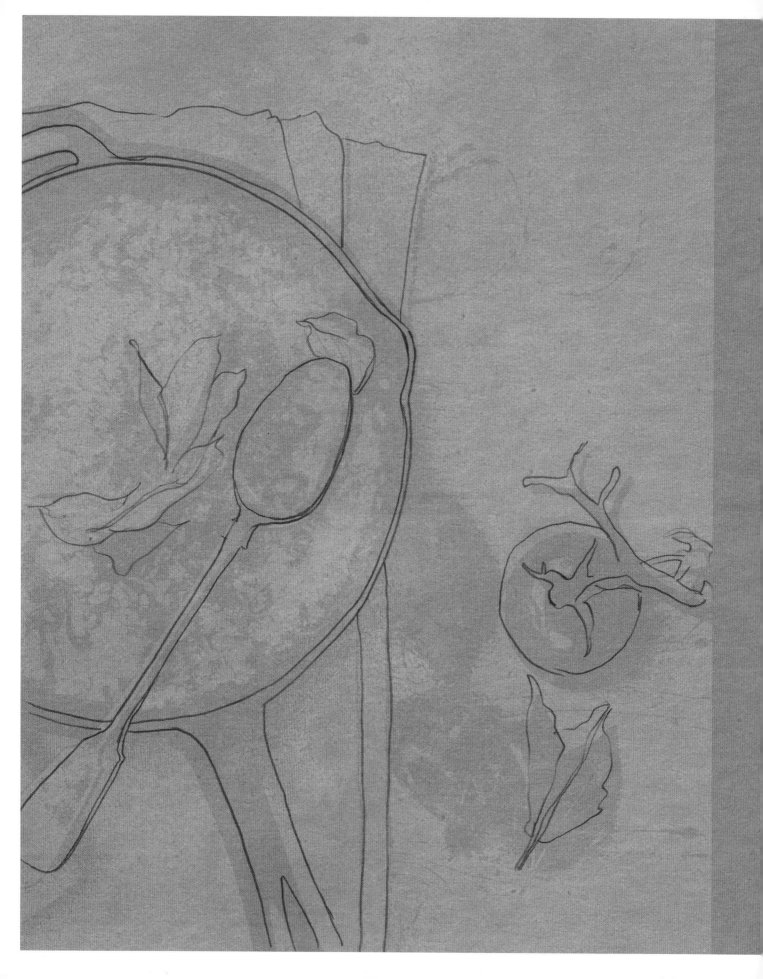

lunchtime

In my mind, there are two types of lunches: the quick weekday lunch you take to work or eat on the run, and the leisurely lunch you can take time preparing and eating with friends and family. I love both, which is why I've put the quick and easy recipes at the front of this chapter and the more leisurely recipes towards the back. The leisurely, or 'lazy', lunches aren't complicated, but they may require longer cooking times or a bit more preparation than the quick recipes. When you have a whole Saturday or Sunday to relax and enjoy your time in the kitchen, putting a little more effort into a meal isn't a problem. Many of my all-time favourite lunch recipes have popped up in this chapter, they are dishes that I make often and they always hit the spot.

Hands down, this would have to be my favourite salad to make at home. It was taught to me by a good mate and wonderful chef, John Pye, who worked alongside me for a number of years. The beauty of this dish lies in its simplicity: fresh ripe figs, amazing quality buffalo mozzarella from Italy and gorgeous fresh basil leaves all lightly coated with one of the most amazing dressings I have come across: apple balsamic. You should be able to track some down at good delis, or online. This is amazing as it is, but if you want to send it off the Richter scale, try adding some paper-thin slices of Ibérico ham or some great quality prosciutto or capacolla from a trusted small goods supplier. You must try this!

fig, basil, buffalo mozzarella & apple balsamic salad

SERVES 4

Tear the figs and mozzarella in half and arrange on a platter with the basil leaves. Drizzle with the olive oil and season with salt and pepper.

Tear the ham and scatter over the salad. Drizzle the apple balsamic over the top.

8 fresh figs
2 balls of Italian buffalo mozzarella (blue cheese or bocconcini can be used instead)
16 basil leaves
lemon-infused extra virgin olive oil
8 slices jamón Ibérico, prosciutto or cappacolla
apple balsamic vinegar (or aged balsamic is fine)

I never get tired of cooking this salad at home when I have friends over. It has everything I like in a dish — it is quick, simple, tasty and quite good for you. It really makes a lovely lunch or starter. If you want to make it into more of a meal, toast some sourdough, break it into pieces and mix with the tomatoes, or simply toss some cooked pasta through the salad.

Warm asparagus salad with buffalo mozzarella & cherry tomatoes

SERVES 4

20 green asparagus spears
150 ml (5 fl oz) extra virgin olive oil
6 garlic cloves, peeled and sliced
14 cherry tomatoes, cut in half
15 black olives, pitted and cut in half
juice of 2 lemons
1 handful of flat-leaf (Italian) parsley, chopped
2 balls of Italian buffalo mozzarella, cut in half
pinch of chilli flakes
2 tablespoons baby purple basil

Blanch the asparagus in boiling water for 2 minutes, then refresh in iced water until the asparagus is cold. Remove from the water and place on paper towel to soak up the excess water.

In a frying pan, heat the olive oil over medium heat, add the garlic and cook until light golden. Add the cherry tomatoes, olives, lemon juice and parsley and cook for 30 seconds, then toss in the asparagus and cook for a further 30 seconds. Season with salt and freshly ground black pepper.

Arrange the asparagus salad on four plates. Top with the mozzarella, then sprinkle with chilli flakes and baby purple basil.

Growing up, the two things I couldn't stand to eat were asparagus and beetroot. Like a lot of Aussies, my first introduction to the humble beetroot was through my love of hamburgers and steak sandwiches and, unfortunately, the beetroot in these would come out of a tin. My aversion to all beetroot stemmed from the taste of the tinned variety, in the same way that tinned asparagus turned me off asparagus for many years. It wasn't until I started working in a professional kitchen that I got to taste my first roasted beetroot ... what a difference! Now I love beetroot how ever it's prepared — roasted, puréed or pickled — and I particularly love this salad, which features beetroot as the star ingredient.

Warm baby beetroot, goat's cheese & walnut salad

SERVES 4–6

Preheat the oven to 180°C (350°F/Gas 4). Trim the beetroot stems, leaving 1 cm (½ inch) intact. Wash the beetroot, place in a baking dish, then sprinkle with thyme, oil, salt and freshly ground black pepper. Tightly cover the dish with foil and roast the beetroot for about 40 minutes, or until tender, shaking the pan after 20 minutes. Remove the beetroot from the dish. When cool enough to touch, peel off the skin.

Meanwhile, place the walnuts on a baking tray. Bake for about 5 minutes or until toasted. Coarsely chop.

Combine the extra virgin olive oil, vinegar, lemon juice and half the walnuts in a small screw-top jar with a little sea salt and freshly ground black pepper. Shake well.

Cut some of the larger beetroot in half lengthways, but leave the smaller beetroot whole, if you prefer.

Thickly spread the goat's cheese out on a large platter and top with the warm beetroot. Drizzle the beetroot with the dressing, then scatter over the chives and season with salt and freshly ground black pepper. Garnish with the remaining walnuts. Serve warm.

2 bunches of baby red and gold beetroot (beets), about 20
½ bunch of thyme
2 tablespoons olive oil
100 g (3½ oz/1 cup) walnuts
80 ml (2½ fl oz/⅓ cup) extra virgin olive oil
2 tablespoons good-quality red wine vinegar
2 teaspoons lemon juice
200 g (7 oz) goat's cheese (chèvre)
1 bunch of chives, cut into 5 cm (2 inch) lengths

I think this is one of the simplest and tastiest recipes I have ever come across. I had this on the menu at Hugos Bondi for ten years and it was the most popular item, which was fantastic for all of us chefs as it was the easiest of all the dishes to cook. Just make sure when you are preparing this recipe that the avocados are ripe and the prawns are fresh. For an even easier version, just buy cooked prawns, peel them and pop them on top of the avocado.

prawn & avocado stack

SERVES 4

1 red capsicum (pepper)
2 avocados, peeled, stoned and diced
1 roma (plum) tomato, seeded and chopped
1 bird's eye chilli, finely chopped
1 tablespoon lemon juice
1 tablespoon chopped coriander (cilantro)
1 tablespoon extra virgin olive oil
2 teaspoons diced red onion
4 teaspoons chilli oil
16 prawns (shrimp), peeled and deveined, leaving tails left intact
2 tablespoons olive oil
2 garlic cloves, peeled and finely chopped
a wedge of lemon, for squeezing

BASIL OIL
1 handful basil leaves
125 ml (4 fl oz/½ cup) olive oil

To make the basil oil, blanch the basil in boiling water and refresh in iced water. Strain the water off and wring out in a clean tea towel (dish cloth) to remove all moisture. Blend with oil in a blender and season to taste.

Preheat the barbecue or grill pan to hot. Cook the capsicum, turning occasionally, for about 15–20 minutes or until the skin turns black. Remove from the barbecue and leave to cool. Peel, seed and remove skin, then finely dice.

Gently mix the avocado, tomato, capsicum, chilli, lemon juice, coriander, olive oil, onion and sea salt and cracked pepper in a bowl. Place a large cookie cutter on a serving plate. Divide the avocado mixture into 4 portions and place one in the cookie cutter. Remove the cutter, drizzle some of the basil and chilli oil around the plate, then repeat with the other 3 plates.

Season the prawns with sea salt and pepper and cook until golden on one side, then turn over and cook until almost done. Add the garlic, a good squeeze of lemon juice and olive oil. Place the prawns onto the avocado stacks and serve immediately.

I was a vegetarian, from when I was 19, for about four years. I needed a change in lifestyle so I did a three-day course on self-improvement and came back changed for the better. I didn't touch alcohol or meat for the next four years, and I really embraced vegetarian cooking and used legumes, nuts, fruit and vegetables to create wonderful meals. I took it very seriously and learned a lot about health and wellbeing in that time. However, I did start to crave meat again and now I have a varied diet. This recipe uses haloumi, a great ingredient to cook on the barbie. I have added some chorizo to spice things up a bit, but you can leave it out if you like and it will still taste wonderful.

grilled haloumi with roasted capsicum, chickpeas & chorizo

SERVES 4

Preheat a barbecue grill or grill pan to high. Cook the capsicums, turning occasionally, for 15–20 minutes, or until the skin turns black. Remove from the barbecue and let cool. Peel, deseed, discard the skins and cut the flesh into strips.

Cook the chorizo until slightly blackened on each side. Add the chorizo to a bowl with the paprika, olive oil, sherry vinegar, parsley leaves, capsicum and chickpeas.

Meanwhile, lightly coat the haloumi with oil and cook on the grill for 1–2 minutes until golden on each side. Season with sea salt, chilli flakes and lemon juice. Add it to the chorizo mixture and toss gently to combine.

4 red capsicums (peppers)
2 chorizo sausages, cut into 5 mm (¼ inch) thick slices
pinch of smoked paprika
4 tablespoons extra virgin olive oil
1 tablespoon sherry or red wine vinegar
1 handful flat-leaf (Italian) parsley
400 g (14 oz) tinned chickpeas, rinsed and drained
250 g (9 oz) haloumi cheese, cut into 5 mm (¼ inch) thick slices
olive oil, for cooking
pinch of chilli flakes
juice of 1 lemon

I love cooking these little crab cakes. I like to think of them as a more grown-up version of potato wedges with sweet chilli and sour cream. A couple of these with a nice big leafy green salad would make a beautiful lunch. Or, if you've got lots of people coming over, knock up a double batch and make slightly smaller cakes to serve as canapés. If you can't get crab, finely chopped prawn or bug meat would also do the trick, but personally I think crabmeat is the big winner.

crab & sweet corn cakes

SERVES 4

200 g (7 oz) cooked crabmeat (either mud, spanner, blue swimmer or tinned)
2 spring onions (scallions), finely sliced
1 long red chilli, finely chopped
1 tablespoon roughly chopped coriander (cilantro)
60 g (2¼ oz/½ cup) plain (all-purpose) flour
60 g (2¼ oz/½ cup) cornflour (cornstarch)
2 free-range eggs, beaten
100 g (3½ oz/½ cup) tinned corn kernels, drained
150 g (5½ oz) crème fraîche or sour cream
sweet chilli sauce, to serve
lime wedges, to serve

Combine the crab, spring onion, chilli and coriander in a bowl and season with salt and freshly ground black pepper.

Sift the flours into a separate bowl. Add 150 ml (5 fl oz) cold water and the eggs and whisk until smooth. Stir in the crab mixture and corn kernels. The mixture should have the consistency of thick cream.

Preheat a large frying pan to medium–high and grease with some oil. Spoon small amounts of the batter into the pan and cook for 3 minutes on each side, or until golden. Serve with crème fraîche, sweet chilli sauce and lime wedges.

Scallops and duck are a beautiful combination in Asian cookery, and this is a very impressive, but easy, dish to make for a quick lunch. Buy yourself a roast Peking duck from Chinatown and shred the meat from the bones (you can also ask for this to be done for you). You then make a very simple stir-fry that is served in a fine omelette with a light broth poured over the top. If you have crabmeat on hand, you could use that instead of the scallops.

scallop & sichuan duck omelette

SERVES 4

To make the miso broth, put all ingredients in a saucepan and bring almost to the boil. Reduce the heat and simmer for 20 minutes, then strain.

Heat the palm sugar (if using) and fish sauce in a small pan until the sugar dissolves. Crack the eggs into a mixing bowl and whisk in the melted palm sugar and fish sauce.

Heat a touch of oil in a non-stick frying pan and pour in just enough of the egg mixture to cover the bottom of the pan. Cook until just golden on the bottom but still moist on top. Slide the omelette out onto a plate and cook another three, using the rest of the eggs.

Heat some oil in a wok and stir-fry the mushrooms. Add the scallops and cook for 10 seconds, then stir in the duck meat. Take off the heat and spoon this filling into the centre of each omelette. Add a few bean sprouts and snow pea sprouts, then roll up the omelette and place in a warm bowl. Ladle hot miso broth over the top, drizzle with kecap manis and sprinkle with spring onions to serve.

NOTE: Kecap manis is a sweet soy sauce from Indonesia. You can usually find it in supermarkets near the other varieties of soy sauce.

1 tablespoon grated palm sugar (jaggery) (optional)
1 tablespoon fish sauce
6 free-range eggs
3 tablespoons coconut or olive oil
8 shiitake mushrooms, sliced
8 Queensland sea scallops, roe removed, cut in half crossways
1 cup roasted Peking duck meat, shredded
a handful of bean sprouts, roughly chopped
a handful of snow pea sprouts, roughly chopped
1 quantity miso broth, see below
4 tablespoons kecap manis (see note)
a few spring onions, julienned

MISO BROTH
MAKES ABOUT 185 ML (6 FL OZ/ ¾ CUP)
250 ml (9 fl oz/1 cup) chicken or fish stock
4 tablespoons orange juice
1 teaspoon finely chopped fresh ginger
2 kaffir lime leaves, torn in half (or a squeeze of lime juice)
1 teaspoon sichuan peppercorns
1 tablespoon kecap manis (see note)
2 teaspoons miso paste

I'm pretty health conscious these days, but I can't deny that this is one of the nicest ways to enjoy firm white-fleshed fish. As long as you drain it well on kitchen paper before serving, it's still fairly healthy — especially if you serve it with some beautiful crunchy vegetables. Like my dad always says, everything is all right in moderation.

fish salad with japanese dressing

SERVES 4

90 g (3 oz/½ cup) rice or coconut flour
90 g (3 oz/½ cup) potato starch or tapioca flour
4 x 160 g (5¾ oz) coral trout fillets, skin on, pinboned, cut into 5 cm (2 inch) pieces
coconut oil, for deep-frying
2 cloves of garlic, peeled and finely sliced
2 handfuls of baby rocket
2 handfuls of baby mizuna leaves
2 handfuls of frisée lettuce leaves
a handful of mint leaves
a handful of coriander leaves
1 long red chilli, julienned
3 tablespoons julienned leek
4 tablespoons salmon roe
1 quantity Japanese salad dressing,
4 tablespoons toasted almond flakes

JAPANESE SALAD DRESSING
3 tablespoons grapeseed oil
2 tablespoons rice wine vinegar
1 teaspoon sliced spring onion, white part only
1 teaspoon English mustard
1 teaspoon light soy sauce
1 teaspoon mirin
a few drops of fish sauce
a pinch of chilli powder

To make the Japanese dressing, either whisk or blend together all the ingredients and season with sea salt and cracked pepper.

Mix together the rice flour and potato starch and use to dust the pieces of coral trout.

Heat the oil to 185°C (365°F) in a deep-fat fryer or large wok — either measure this with a thermometer or drop a cube of bread into the oil: if it bubbles up and turns golden, then the oil is ready. Add the slices of garlic to the oil and fry for a few seconds until the garlic is golden. Use a slotted spoon to transfer the garlic to kitchen paper and leave to drain. Deep-fry the coral trout in batches until golden and crisp. Drain on kitchen paper.

Mix together the greens, herbs, chilli, leek and salmon roe and dress with the salad dressing. Toss the fish through the salad and pile onto four plates. Sprinkle with the crispy garlic chips and the almonds.

One of the best rolls in the world is this one — not even my famous prawn roll can top it! You must try one to believe it. It is based on the beautiful bahn mi rolls you get in places like Sydney's Cabramatta, which has a high concentration of Vietnamese residents, restaurants and bakeries. I have adapted it slightly to be cooked on the barbecue but you could just as easily use roasted chicken from the night before or store-bought barbecued chicken instead. The key here is the pickled carrot and onion and also the delicious flavoured mayonnaise slathered onto the bread. Use the best-quality bread rolls or baguettes you can find or, if you want to leave out the bread completely, just follow the recipe below and turn it into a big, beautiful salad.

vietnamese barbecued chicken salad baguettes

SERVES 4

Combine the vinegar, sugar (if using), ½ teaspoon of salt, garlic and chilli and mix well. Add the grated carrot and sliced onion, mix well and set aside.

Preheat the barbecue hotplate to medium–high. Place the chicken, skin side down, on the barbecue hotplate and cook for 8 minutes or until the skin is golden. Turn over and continue cooking for 5 minutes or until cooked through. Allow to cool, then shred the meat.

Combine the mayonnaise with the lime juice and five-spice and mix well.

Lightly toast the baguettes on the barbecue. Spread the mayonnaise mixture onto one side of the bread. Top with shredded chicken and then with carrot and onion salad. Garnish the roll with chopped coriander, nuts, and chilli.

NOTE: Sambal oelek is an Indonesian chilli paste, available from Asian supermarkets.

2 tablespoons white vinegar
1 teaspoon caster (superfine) sugar (optional)
1 garlic clove, peeled and crushed
1 small red chilli, finely chopped, or 1 teaspoon sambal oelek (see note)
1 large carrot, grated
1 white onion, peeled and finely sliced
4 boneless free-range chicken breasts (skin on)
4 tablespoons mayonnaise
1 tablespoon lime juice
½ teaspoon five-spice
2 baguettes, halved and sliced lengthwise (be careful to not cut all the way through)
1 handful of coriander (cilantro)
4 tablespoons roasted and chopped cashews or peanuts
1 long red chilli, finely chopped

This is a classic Thai recipe that's a winner when you want to either start the meal with something light and tasty, or go for a light lunch. The beauty of this, apart from its simplicity and flavour, is its texture. The rice is fried in its raw state until it turns golden brown and then crushed with a mortar and pestle and incorporated into the most aromatic salad you can imagine. This gives the salad a great textural crunch that is quite unique. I love to eat this wrapped in fresh cabbage leaves — a Thai version of san choy bau.

chicken larb salad

SERVES 4 (AS A STARTER)

2 tablespoons uncooked jasmine rice
500 g (1 lb 2 oz) boneless, skinless, free-range chicken breast, minced
2 tablespoons cornflour
2 tablespoons coconut or olive oil
4 tablespoons lime juice
2 tablespoons fish sauce
1 small red chilli, deseeded and finely chopped
4 red Asian shallots, peeled and diced
½ bunch of spring onions (scallions) (green part only), finely sliced
1 large handful of coriander (cilantro) leaves, torn
1 small handful of Thai basil, leaves torn
1 large handful of mint leaves, torn
fresh cabbage or lettuce leaves, to serve
cucumber and green beans, to serve

Add the rice to a wok or frying pan over medium–high heat and cook, shaking the pan continuously, for about 2–3 minutes or until the rice is golden and toasted. Remove from the pan and leave to cool.

Grind the rice in a spice grinder or mortar and pestle until it has a coarse texture (not too fine).

Lightly coat the chicken mince in the cornflour. Wipe out the frying pan with kitchen paper and heat over medium–high heat. Add a little oil and cook the mince, breaking it up with your spoon and stirring frequently for 2–3 minutes until cooked and crumbly.

Stir in the lime juice, fish sauce, chilli, shallots and spring onions. Leave to cool for 1 minute.

Toss the coriander, Thai basil, mint and ground rice through the chicken mince. Taste for seasoning and serve with fresh cabbage or lettuce leaves, sliced cucumber and green beans.

Certain dishes can take me back to a specific time and place in my life, and this is definitely one of them. On my first visit to Vietnam I had the most amazing time eating my way around the country via the local street stalls. If you've never shopped at an Asian grocery store, this salad is a great one to go shopping for because there are a few special ingredients to hunt down. You may think it's a little extravagant that I'm asking you to buy two different types of mint and track down banana flowers, but it's these little touches that give the salad its authenticity.

vietnamese banana flower salad

SERVES 4

Remove three or four outer layers of the banana flower until you get to the whitish part (not the purple part). Cut off the bottom core and the tip, then cut crossways into thin strips until you get to the bottom (do not use the small banana-looking fingers at the bottom of each leaf — discard them). Put the banana flower strips into some cold water with a bit of lemon or lime juice added to stop them discolouring, and leave for 10 minutes.

Using a mortar and pestle or food processor, pound or process the chilli, ginger, garlic and sugar. Add the lime juice, fish sauce and 2 tablespoons of water.

Combine the drained banana flower, bean sprouts, prawns, green papaya, cucumber, chilli, coriander leaves, Asian shallots, Thai basil and the mint leaves in a large bowl. Add the dressing, to taste.

To make the crispy shallots, put the shallots and oil in a small saucepan and heat until the shallots start to turn golden. Lift out with a slotted spoon and drain on kitchen paper.

Serve the salad on a platter, topped with toasted peanuts and some crispy shallots.

SALAD

1 large or 2 small banana flowers
100 g (3½ oz/1 cup) bean sprouts
200 g (7 oz) cooked prawns (shrimp), peeled and deveined, tails intact
1 green papaya, peeled and julienned
1 cucumber, seeded and julienned
1 long red chilli, deseeded and julienned
3 red Asian shallots, peeled and finely sliced
1 small handful each of Thai basil, coriander, Vietnamese mint and mint leaves
1 handful of unsalted peanuts, roasted and chopped

DRESSING

2–3 small hot red chillies, finely diced
1 teaspoon grated ginger
2 garlic cloves, peeled and minced
2 tablespoons caster (superfine) sugar (optional)
4 tablespoons lime juice
2 tablespoons fish sauce

CRISPY SHALLOTS

4 French shallots, peeled and thinly sliced
500 ml (17 fl oz/2 cups) olive or coconut oil

I love the way that Australia has embraced the foods of other nationalities with such conviction and open arms. In Bondi, where I live, we have Thai, Chinese, Vietnamese, Mexican, Russian, Portuguese, French, Italian, Indian, Japanese, Korean, Spanish, Lebanese and Turkish restaurants to name just a few. Not only do we choose to go out and eat a variety of cuisines, we also stay home and cook them for ourselves. Long gone are the days of meat and three veg on a table every night. Now we cook up a quick stir-fry, slow braised tagine or even a lovely curry. This recipe is a great one to cook on the barbecue (or in a pan) and present to family and friends when they come over as it pleases everyone. It's perfectly balanced with the steak, fresh herbs and noodles without being too filling.

thai beef salad

SERVES 4

3 tablespoons sea salt

3 tablespoons cracked black peppercorns

600 g (1 lb 5 oz) eye fillet (1 long piece preferable)

olive oil, for cooking

100 g (3½ oz) rice vermicelli noodles

3 spring onions (scallions), thinly sliced on the diagonal

1 small handful of Thai basil leaves

1 small handful of mint leaves

1 small handful of coriander (cilantro) leaves

2 tablespoons chopped roasted peanuts

DRESSING

2 tablespoons finely diced ginger

2 tablespoons peeled and finely chopped coriander (cilantro) stems

3 garlic cloves, peeled and chopped

1 large red chilli, thinly sliced

1 tablespoon grated palm sugar (jaggery) or soft brown sugar

2 tablespoons rice vinegar

2 tablespoons soy sauce

1 tablespoon finely chopped lemongrass (white part only)

4 tablespoons extra virgin olive oil

Preheat the barbecue hotplate or grill pan to high. Put the salt and pepper on a tray and roll the beef fillet in it evenly. Rub some olive oil all over the beef and cook it for 4–5 minutes on each side until seared all over and rare inside. Rest for 10 minutes before slicing (or place into the fridge and let cool before slicing).

Place the noodles in a bowl and pour over some boiling water. Set aside until tender. Rinse and drain.

To make the dressing, combine the ginger, coriander, garlic, chilli, sugar (if using), vinegar, soy, lemongrass, sesame oil and olive oil in a bowl. Pour half the dressing over the noodles.

To serve, place the noodles on a platter and top with the beef slices, then top with the spring onions, herbs, remaining dressing and the peanuts and toss to combine. You can serve this dish at room temperature or cold.

Pho is generally eaten for breakfast in Vietnam but I find it is good at any time of the day: brekky, lunch or dinner. Pho is a meal in itself — you won't need anything else if you have this. When I travelled through Vietnam a few years ago, I ate this dish nearly every day, and it was different each time. The main thing to remember here is that this dish is all about the broth, so take the time to make it properly. You can also freeze the broth, so if you make a big batch you won't have to do it again for a while.

vietnamese pho

To make the broth, wrap the spices in a piece of muslin (cheesecloth) and secure with string so you have a little flavour bag.

In a large stockpot, cook off the onion and ginger in a touch of oil until they get a bit of colour; once coloured, add the water, bones, gravy beef and flavour bag and simmer for 2–3 hours, frequently skimming any scum from the surface. Once the beef is tender, season the broth with the salt, fish sauce and sugar. Allow to cool, then strain into a large bowl, reserving the beef and any bones. Discard the rest.

Once the meat is cool enough to handle, remove the oxtail meat from the bones and dice the flesh; shred the gravy meat and place both in a bowl.

Return the broth to the pot and return to the boil. If you are using fresh noodles, blanch them for 20 seconds, then drain. If you are using dried noodles, cook in boiling water for 2–3 minutes, or until just tender, then drain. Fill each serving bowl with some rice noodles, cooked and raw beef, then top with the boiling broth, sprouts, herbs and sauces. Top with chilli and serve with lime wedges on the side.

SERVES 6

BROTH
1 piece cassia bark or 1 cinnamon stick
1 tablespoon coriander seeds
1 tablespoon fennel seeds
4 star anise
3 cardamom pods
5 whole cloves
2 onions, peeled and halved
3 tablespoons sliced fresh ginger
olive oil
5 litres (20 cups) water
400 g (14 oz) oxtail or other beef bones, cut into 5 cm (2 inch) pieces
800 g (1 lb 12 oz) gravy beef, such as flank
1½ tablespoons sea salt
70 ml (2¼ fl oz) fish sauce
2.5 cm (1 inch) chunk of yellow rock sugar or white sugar)

TO SERVE
300 g (10½ oz) thick fresh or dried rice noodles
200 g (7 oz) eye fillet or sirloin beef (wagyu, if possible), very thinly sliced
100 g (3½ oz) bean sprouts, trimmed
1 large handful each of mint, coriander (cilantro), Thai basil and sliced spring onion (scallion)
80 ml (2½ fl oz/⅓ cup) hoisin sauce
Sriracha hot chilli sauce (optional)
2–3 bird's eye chillies, thinly sliced
2 limes, cut into wedges

Here is a simple pasta dish that has just a few ingredients: cherry tomatoes, garlic (lots of it), chilli, anchovies and fresh herbs — I tend to alternate between basil and parsley. If I'm using parsley I fry it into the sauce at the start, but if I'm using basil, I tear it into the pasta at the last minute. Sometimes I pop capers or olives in here, or finish it with rocket or spinach and a squeeze of lemon. You can also make it with a fresh, uncooked tomato sauce: just make a dressing, crush the cherry tomatoes with a potato masher and add basil and cooked pasta for a light summer lunch. It's one of those dishes that changes every time I cook it — that's exactly what I love about it.

cherry tomato pasta

SERVES 4

150 ml (5½ fl oz) extra virgin olive oil
10 garlic cloves, peeled and thinly sliced
2 bird's eye chillies, finely chopped
6 anchovies
1 tablespoon capers, drained
2 punnets of cherry tomatoes, halved
2 tablespoons white wine
1 small handful of basil leaves
400 g (14 oz) dried orecchiette or any pasta you like
juice of ½ lemon
shaved parmesan cheese, to serve

Combine the oil, garlic, chilli and anchovies in a pan over medium–low heat until the garlic starts to turn a light brown colour. Break down the anchovies with a wooden spoon.

Add the capers, tomatoes and white wine and season with salt and pepper. Cook for another 3 minutes, then stir in the basil.

Meanwhile, cook the pasta in boiling salted water according to the packet instructions, then drain. Add to the sauce and toss well. Stir in the lemon juice and serve with the shaved parmesan.

As well as being a warming meal for a winter lunch or dinner, risotto also makes a great dish to serve at a party once all the finger food has been consumed. A large pot of risotto will be enough for many small bowls and it will leave your guests feeling satisfied. Choose your favourite risotto recipe and the one you are most confident and proud of serving. This is one of my favourite risottos as it is full of flavour and colour.

pumpkin & borlotti bean risotto

SERVES 4

Preheat the oven to 180°C (350°F/Gas 4). To make the risotto, heat the oil in a saucepan over medium heat. Add the celery, onion, oregano, chilli and cinnamon stick and cook until the celery and onion are soft but not coloured. Add the rice and stir well so the rice gets coated in the oil, then add the stock. Bring to the boil then turn down to a simmer, stirring continuously, until the liquid has almost evaporated and the rice is cooked. Remove from the stovetop.

Meanwhile, place the pumpkin on a roasting tray and sprinkle with the oregano and some salt and freshly ground black pepper, then drizzle with the oil. Roast for 10–15 minutes, or until soft.

Once the pumpkin is tender, mash it using a potato masher. Add the pumpkin to the risotto and return the risotto to the stovetop over low–medium heat. Stir well. Add the pasta sauce and butter and stir until combined, adding a splash more extra stock if needed. Add the borlotti beans and stir well. Season.

To finish, place a good portion of risotto on a plate or serving dish, top with grated parmesan and garnish with diced tomato mixed with the lemon juice, oil and basil.

RISOTTO

1 tablespoon olive oil
½ celery stalk, finely diced
¼ red onion, finely diced
1 tablespoon dried oregano
½ teaspoon chilli flakes
1 cinnamon stick
200 g (7 oz) arborio rice
600 ml (21 fl oz) hot vegetable stock, plus extra

PUMPKIN

400 g (14 oz) pumpkin (winter squash), peeled, seeds removed and cut into 2 cm (¾ inch) dice
1 teaspoon dried oregano
2 tablespoons olive oil

3 tablespoons passata
30 g (1 oz) butter
100 g (3½ oz) tinned borlotti beans, rinsed and drained
70 g (2½ oz/½ cup) freshly grated parmesan
1 vine-ripened tomato, seeds removed and diced
1 tablespoon lemon juice
3 tablespoons extra virgin olive oil
1 small handful of basil leaves

If you have been to a farmers' market or visited a festival lately you may have the noticed the queues around one stall in particular… the gozleme stall. These delicious Turkish-style filled 'pizzas' are one of my all-time favourite fast foods, and I love watching them being rolled out by the ladies in their white uniforms and hair nets. There are a few classic fillings such as spinach and cheese, and my favourite: meat and spinach. The thing to remember when cooking is to get them golden brown and then smother them in fresh lemon juice. The kids love them, too. I reckon the first person to franchise these things is going to make a fortune.

gozleme of lamb, mint, feta & spinach with lemon

SERVES 4

200 g (7 oz) plain yoghurt
250 g (9 oz/2 cups) self-raising flour
1 tablespoon olive oil
150 g (5½ oz) minced lamb
1 garlic clove, peeled and crushed
a pinch of ground cumin
a pinch of chilli flakes
a pinch of dried mint
4 tablespoons tomato juice
50 g (1¾ oz) baby English spinach
100 g (3½ oz) feta cheese, crumbled
8 mint leaves, torn
olive oil, for frying
50 g (1¾ oz) butter, melted (optional)
lemon wedges, to serve

Beat the yoghurt and a pinch of salt in a large bowl until smooth. Gradually add flour until it is a stiff dough. Tip onto a lightly floured bench and gradually knead the dough, incorporating any remaining flour until it is soft and only slightly sticky. Transfer to an oiled bowl and leave, covered, for 30 minutes.

Heat the oil in a frying pan and cook the lamb with a pinch of salt and pepper until browned. Turn the heat down to medium–low and add the garlic, cumin, chilli flakes and tomato juice. Cook for another minute or until dry. Turn off the heat and leave to cool, then drain.

On a floured surface, split the dough into four equal balls. Roll each ball into a 30 cm (12 inch) circle. Place a quarter of the spinach over half of each circle, then sprinkle with a quarter of the feta, then add the lamb and mint leaves and season. Fold the dough over and seal the edges with a fork.

Preheat a barbecue hotplate or large frying pan. Brush one side of each gozleme with olive oil and cook until the base is golden. Brush the top with olive oil, turn and cook until golden.

Brush with melted butter, cut into four pieces and serve with a pinch of sea salt and some lemon wedges.

This is a really easy way of feeding a crowd at your next barbie without going down the old sausage in bread with tomato sauce route (even though I adore grilled sausages. This recipe is a celebration of healthy ingredients: chicken, fresh herbs, yoghurt and Lebanese bread, all wrapped up like they do in the kebab shops.

chicken shawarma with yoghurt & garlic

SERVES 4

Preheat the barbecue grill to medium–high. Combine the lemon juice, oil, spices, a pinch of salt and coriander in a large bowl. Add the chicken and toss to coat.

Cook the chicken on the grill for 4–5 minutes on each side, or until cooked through. Shred with a sharp knife.

Meanwhile, to make the yoghurt and garlic sauce, blend the garlic, 2 teaspoons of salt and lemon juice in a blender until smooth. Gradually add the oil in a thin steady stream while the motor is still running, until the sauce has thickened, then fold in the yoghurt and sumac.

To make the tabouleh combine the parsley, tomato and onion.

To assemble, place Lebanese bread on the grill for about 5–10 seconds to warm, then spread with the yoghurt and garlic sauce. Arrange the tabouleh, lettuce and chicken on top. Roll up to enclose and cut in half to serve.

3 tablespoons lemon juice
2 tablespoons olive oil
2 teaspoons ground allspice
1 tablespoon ground coriander
3 tablespoons chopped coriander (cilantro)
1 kg (2 lb 4 oz) boneless, skinless, free-range chicken thigh fillets, fat trimmed
6 white Lebanese breads, warmed
2 large handfuls of shredded iceberg lettuce

YOGHURT & GARLIC SAUCE
8 garlic cloves, peeled
3 tablespoons lemon juice
300 ml (10½ fl oz) olive oil
125 g (4½ oz/½ cup) plain yoghurt
2 teaspoons sumac

QUICK TABOULEH
3 handfuls of flat-leaf (Italian) parsley, chopped
1 vine-ripened tomato, diced
¼ small onion, peeled and sliced

Udo, my best mate, and I were hunting the elusive jungle perch in Far North Queensland and I had this recipe in mind after a recent trip to Thailand. However, after talking to the locals about the fragility of the jungle perch population, we couldn't bring ourselves to eat the one that we'd amazingly managed to catch. Luckily we ran into some aboriginal men who had speared a blue-tail mullet and offered to share (it was a bloody big fish). So I substituted the mullet for the perch (a little like substituting a Kombi van for a Ferrari). The end result was nothing short of a culinary masterpiece. You could also use any firm white-fleshed fish, crab, prawns, scallop, lobster or bugs.

ho mok pla (steamed fish curry)

SERVES 4 AS A STARTER

200 g (7 oz) blue-tailed mullet fillet, skin and bones removed
2 free-range eggs
3 tablespoons coconut milk
1 tablespoon fish sauce
1 tablespoon grated palm sugar (jaggery), melted (optional)
1–2 teaspoons red curry paste
1 tablespoon finely sliced kaffir lime leaf
1 chilli, finely chopped
juice of 1 lime
8 banana leaf or baking paper crosses, cut from 25 cm (12 inch) squares
10 Thai basil or coriander leaves

Finely dice the fish and place in a chilled bowl. Mix together the eggs, coconut milk, fish sauce, palm sugar, curry paste, kaffir lime leaf, chilli and lime juice and then stir through the diced fish.

Lay a banana leaf cross on your bench top, shiny side down, and fold three arms of the cross together to make a pouch. Spoon the fish mixture into the pouches, with a few leaves of Thai basil. Fold the last arm over to make a parcel and secure with short bamboo skewers.

Put the parcels in a steamer over simmering water and steam for about 5 minutes or until the fish is cooked through (open a parcel to check — it should look like a just-set custard). Cut open the parcels and serve with lime wedges and crispy shallots.

This is a style of food I so love to eat and also cook. A beautiful piece of fish that you have either caught or bought, married with a light flavoursome salsa that only takes a matter of minutes to put together. The best thing of all is that it's delicious and healthy, so you know you are doing yourself and your guests a favour by cooking it. I'm using a cheat's ingredient here: jarred artichoke hearts. You can buy them in grocery stores and good delis, and they really do make this so quick and easy to prepare.

barbecued fish with an italian garden salsa of artichokes & tomato

SERVES 4

To make the salsa, cut the tomatoes into quarters and discard the seeds. Finely dice the tomato flesh and artichokes and place in a bowl. Add the olives, parsley and pine nuts, then add the oil and lemon juice and season with salt and pepper.

Preheat the barbecue hotplate to high. Brush the fish with some oil and cook on the hotplate for a few minutes on each side, depending on how thick the fish is. Serve with the salsa.

4 vine-ripened tomatoes
150 g (5½ oz) jar preserved artichokes, drained
100 g (3½ oz) pitted kalamata olives
1 handful of flat-leaf (Italian) parsley, chopped
30 g (1 oz) pine nuts, toasted
150 ml (5 fl oz) extra virgin olive oil
juice of 1 lemon
4 x 180 g (6½ oz) fish fillets such as snapper, bream, kingfish or flathead, skin on and pinboned
olive oil, for cooking

I still remember the first time I ate this dish—it was the beautiful texture of the chicken that has stayed with me. The chicken is poached whole, then steeped so the flesh becomes soft and silky. You can serve it with various dipping sauces. Here I have matched it with the traditional ginger and spring onion dressing to keep it Chinese but it works just as well with a South-east Asian dressing and a crunchy green salad.

White-cut chicken (hainanese chicken) with spring onion dressing

SERVES 6

DRESSING
80 ml (2½ fl oz/⅓ cup) peanut oil
4 dried red chillies
2 spring onions (scallions), finely sliced, reserving the green for the garnish
1 large knob of fresh ginger, diced
2 garlic cloves, finely chopped
3 tablespoons Chinese rice wine
100 ml (3½ fl oz) rice vinegar
1 tablespoon salt
1 tablespoon caster (superfine) sugar

1 x 1.6 kg (3 lb 8 oz) free-range organic chicken
3 litres (12 cups) water

RELISH
125 ml (4 fl oz/½ cup) white wine vinegar
115 g (4 oz/½ cup) caster (superfine) sugar (optional)
170 ml (5½ fl oz/⅔ cup) water
2 Lebanese (short) cucumbers, washed, quartered lengthways and sliced (about 1 cup)
8 red Asian shallots
⅓ cup julienned fresh ginger
1 long red chilli, thinly sliced

To make the dressing, heat the oil in a wok over medium heat and cook the chillies until blackened. Discard the chillies and leave the oil to cool. In a bowl, combine the spring onion, ginger, garlic, rice wine, vinegar, salt and sugar, then add to the cooled oil. Leave to stand for 1 hour to allow the flavours to infuse into the oil.

Meanwhile, remove the fat from the cavity of the chicken, rinse the chicken in cold water and pat dry with paper towel. In a saucepan large enough to fit the chicken, bring the water to a boil. Place the chicken into the pan and return to the boil. Place a lid on top of the pan and simmer for 15 minutes.

Meanwhile make the relish. Combine the vinegar, sugar and water in a small saucepan and bring to the boil. Remove from the heat when the sugar has dissolved. Set aside to cool. Mix the remaining ingredients in a bowl and pour the syrup over the top.

Remove the pan with the chicken from the heat and leave the chicken to steep for 20 minutes. During this time do not remove the lid or the heat will be lost and the chicken will not cook. After 20 minutes, remove the lid and carefully lift the chicken from the stock. Drain on paper towel and chop Chinese–style through the bone, then put on a platter.

Pour the spring onion dressing over the chicken, garnish with the green spring onion pieces and serve with the relish and rice.

I love a dish like this one where there are only a few good-quality ingredients. This is a wonderful meal that is perfect for lunch or dinner when you don't want to spend too much time in the kitchen. It is also a great way of eating one of my favourite ingredients, silverbeet. If you prefer, you can substitute cavolo nero, English spinach or broccolini for the silverbeet.

pappardelle with silverbeet, pine nuts & goat's cheese

SERVES 4

Heat the olive oil in a frying pan, add the garlic and cook until lightly golden, then add the onion and cook for a further 3 minutes or until tender. Add the silverbeet and 80 ml (2½ fl oz/⅓ cup) of water and cook for a further 3 minutes, or until the silverbeet is wilted and tender. Season with a good amount of salt and freshly ground black pepper to taste.

Meanwhile, cook the pappardelle in a large saucepan of boiling water until al dente. Drain.

Add the cooked pappardelle to the frying pan with the silverbeet, then add the parsley, pine nuts and extra virgin olive oil and toss until combined.

Divide among four dishes and add a spoonful of goat's cheese to the top of each serving, then add some grated lemon zest, a squeeze of lemon juice, chilli flakes, if using, and some freshly ground black pepper.

NOTE: If you are unable to find fresh pappardelle, you could use dried. You could also use ricotta, blue cheese or buffalo mozzarella instead of the goat's cheese.

125 ml (4 fl oz/½ cup) olive oil
4 garlic cloves, peeled and chopped
1 large onion, peeled and diced
300 g (10½ oz) silverbeet (Swiss chard) leaves, shredded
400 g (14 oz) fresh pappardelle (see note)
⅓ cup chopped flat-leaf (Italian) parsley
50 g (1¾ oz/⅓ cup) pine nuts, toasted
125 ml (4 fl oz/½ cup) extra virgin olive oil
100 g (3½ oz) fresh goat's cheese or goat's curd (see note)
juice and zest of 1 lemon
2 pinches of chilli flakes (optional)

This dish is based on one that was cooked for me by two amazing Italian cooks, Daniela and Stefania. They cooked marinated baby goat with braised cabbage and roasted kipfler potatoes — it was so moreish and flavoursome that I had a smile from ear to ear. This recipe is based on theirs but I have changed the goat to lamb and left out the cabbage. However, if you are cooking for a crowd and want to make things go a little further, you could always shred half a cabbage and add it to the ragu for the last 20 minutes of cooking. If you wanted to enjoy a gluten-free version of this, you could substitute potato for the pasta, and it would be equally as enjoyable. Thank-you for the inspiration, girls!

lamb ragu with rigatoni

SERVES 4–6

MARINADE
1 litre (35 fl oz/4 cups) dry white wine
2 tablespoons extra virgin olive oil
250 ml (9 fl oz/1 cup) chicken stock
2 red onions, peeled and sliced
150 g (5½ oz) semi-dried (sun-blushed) tomatoes, chopped
4 dried bay leaves
½ bunch of thyme, chopped
½ bunch of sage, chopped

1 lamb shoulder on the bone 1.5–2 kg (3 lb 5 oz–4 lb 8 oz), cut into three pieces (ask your butcher to do this)
1 tablespoon olive oil
2 lemons, cut in half
75 g (2½ oz/1 cup) shredded white cabbage (optional)
60 g (2¼ oz) chopped butter
500 g (1 lb 2 oz) rigatoni
1 bunch of flat-leaf (Italian) parsley, finely shredded
freshly grated pecorino, to serve

To make the marinade, combine the wine, extra virgin olive oil, stock, onion, tomato, bay leaves, thyme, sage and some salt and freshly ground black pepper in a large non-reactive bowl.

Rub the marinade all over the lamb pieces, cover and leave in the fridge to marinate for a minimum of 2 hours, preferably overnight if time permits.

Preheat the oven to 150°C (300°F/Gas 2). Drain the meat and onion from the marinade, reserving the liquid.

Heat the olive oil in a flameproof casserole dish over medium–high heat until smoking. Add the meat and turn occasionally for 3–5 minutes until browned. Add the onion to the casserole dish and sauté for 10–12 minutes until starting to caramelise. Add the remaining marinade to the casserole dish. Squeeze over the juice from the lemons and add the lemon halves to the casserole dish. Bring to the boil.

Cover tightly with baking paper, cover with a lid and bake for 1½ hours, then remove the lemons. Add the cabbage, if using, and continue cooking for a further 1–1½ hours until the meat is tender and almost falls from the bone. You may need to add a little water as you are cooking if the liquid reduces too much.

Remove the lamb pieces and bay leaves from the sauce and, when cool enough to handle, break the meat into bite-sized pieces, discarding the bones. Skim off and discard the oil, then return the meat to the sauce. Mix in the butter and season with salt and freshly ground black pepper.

Meanwhile, cook the pasta in a large saucepan of boiling salted water until al dente. Drain. Add the lamb liquor to the pasta, then fold in the meat and most of the parsley. Top with grated pecorino and the remaining parsley.

One of the most important lessons I've learned in my twenty-plus years as a chef is that the simplest things in life are often the best, and nowhere is this truer than in the world of food. How many times have you eaten a beautiful ripe mango or a piece of cold watermelon on a hot summer's day, or caught a fish and cooked it simply with butter, lemon and parsley? I was once working with a world famous chef, recreating his food for a huge event, and we had to substitute a vegetarian option for one of his courses. This eggplant parmigiana was what we offered, and we made quite a bit in case there was a horde of vegetarians. At the end of the night all the staff feasted on leftover parmigiana, and it was unanimously (although quietly!) agreed that everyone liked the simple eggplant parmigiana better than the world-famous chef's fancier dishes. So, please cook this and enjoy the simple things in life.

eggplant parmigiana

SERVES 4

To make the tomato sauce, heat the oil in a saucepan and cook the garlic until it's starting to colour. Add the tomatoes and 125 ml (4 fl oz/ ½ cup) of water and simmer for 20–25 minutes. Add the basil and cook for another 5 minutes. Season to taste and blend until smooth.

To make the parmigiana, preheat the oven to 200°C (400°F/Gas 6). Cut the eggplant into 2 cm (¾ inch) thick slices. Place on oiled baking trays, sprinkle with salt and bake for 20 minutes or until golden.

To put the parmigiana together you'll need to use half the tomato sauce — keep the rest for serving. Line a baking dish or loaf tin with baking paper, brush with oil and make layers, each time using a little of the eggplant, tomato sauce, parmesan, mozzarella and basil. Repeat until you have about five layers, using the slices of egg in only the centre layer.

Lay a sheet of baking paper and then a smaller tray on top and weigh down (perhaps with a heavy ovenproof dish). Bake for 20 minutes at 160°C (315°F/Gas 2–3). Leave to cool with the weight still in place. When cool, turn out of the dish to slice. Reheat in the oven, if you like, and serve on hot Italian tomato sauce with more of the grated parmesan.

ITALIAN TOMATO SAUCE
2 tablespoons olive oil
50 g (1¾ oz) garlic, peeled and thinly sliced
500 g (1 lb 2 oz) tinned tomatoes, crushed
8 basil leaves
4 large eggplants (aubergines)

1 quantity of Italian tomato sauce (see above)
200 ml (7 fl oz) olive oil
200 g (7 oz) grated parmesan
500 g (1 lb 2 oz) Italian buffalo mozzarella, torn into pieces
2 handfuls of basil leaves
4 hard-boiled free-range eggs, peeled and sliced

Stracciatella is a classic Roman egg-drop soup that loosely translates as 'little rags' (because when you whisk the egg and parmesan into the hot broth it looks like torn rags). I have taken the liberty of adding some cavolo nero for texture and also some lardo for added flavour. If you want to make a more substantial meal of this dish, just add some small risoni pasta and some shredded roast chicken.

stracciatella soup with cavolo nero & lardo

SERVES 4

1 litre (35 fl oz/4 cups) chicken stock
100 g (3½ oz) cavolo nero (dark Italian cabbage) or spinach
4 free-range eggs
75 g (2½ oz/¾ cup) grated parmesan
2 teaspoons lemon juice
4 tablespoons chopped parsley
12 thin slices of lardo (cured pork fat), if you like, or extra virgin olive oil, to drizzle

Bring the chicken stock to the boil in a saucepan. Blanch the cavolo nero in the stock for 30 seconds, then take out and roughly chop.

Beat the eggs, parmesan, lemon juice and parsley together with a fork. Pour into the stock and stir for 1 minute, then add the cavolo nero and season with salt and pepper. Serve topped with the lardo or olive oil.

things with drinks

Catering for weddings and other special events is one of the aspects of my job that I love the most. I really enjoy working with clients on menus and themes, and I love the rush of adrenaline I get at the beginning of a party, the race behind the scenes once the guests arrive and, of course, the relief at the end when everything has come together and you know the room is full of happy guests. It's always so rewarding, and the more you do it, the more tricks you have up your sleeve. These next two chapters are for everyone who feels anxiety or pressure when they entertain. Many of these recipes have become my 'go-to' dishes for big events, so I know from experience that they will leave big smiles on your guests' faces. Especially if you serve them with some strong cocktails!

I go fishing in the Northern Territory every year and always pop into my favourite restaurant in Darwin, Hanuman. It's owned by Jimmy Shu and offers a mix of Malay, Indian and Thai cuisines. One dish I always order is the Hanuman oysters. They are cooked with a mix of lemongrass, lime juice, fish sauce and palm sugar along with a few other aromatics. Although I am an oyster purist and love them freshly shucked with nothing, this recipe easily does them more than justice.

hanuman's signature oysters with lemongrass, sweet basil, chilli & fresh coriander

MAKES 20

Cut roots and 5 cm (2 inches) of the stems from the coriander and chop finely, reserving the leaves. Finely chop the basil stems. Process the roots and stems, galangal, lemongrass, chilli, garlic, lime juice, fish sauce and palm sugar (if using) in a food processor until finely chopped. Check for the balance of sweet, sour, salty and hot and adjust if necessary.

Preheat the oven to 200°C (400°F/Gas 6). Place the oysters on a baking tray lined with rock salt and cook for 1 minute or until warm (you could do this under a hot grill (broiler) if you like). Drizzle each oyster with a teaspoon of sauce, scatter with the basil and coriander leaves and serve with the remaining sauce on the side.

2 coriander stalks, roots attached
1 sweet basil stalk, leaves removed
  and stems reserved
½ teaspoon finely grated galangal
2 tablespoons thinly sliced
  lemongrass, white part only
1 small red chilli, finely chopped
1 garlic clove, peeled and finely
  chopped
60 ml (2 fl oz/¼ cup) lime juice
30 ml (1 fl oz) fish sauce
2 tablespoons grated palm
  sugar (jaggery) (optional)
20 Pacific oysters, freshly shucked
  in the shell
rock salt

A few years ago I found myself in LA cooking with Curtis Stone and the legendary Wolfgang Puck's catering team for 'G'Day USA'. We had to cater for 800 people and the following recipe is one of the canapés I created for the night. When I serve this at a function, I normally present the fish salad on betel leaves (edible leaves from South-East Asia that have medicinal qualities). However, on arrival in LA, I found that betel leaves weren't available, so I decided to serve the fish on crispy fried won tons as an alternative. To be honest, I think the won tons worked better as they are easier to handle and add great texture to the end result. For a larger serving, just add some finely sliced green mango, papaya or glass noodles for a refreshing salad.

smoked fish salad on crispy won tons

MAKES 20

coconut or olive oil, for deep-frying
20 won ton wrappers
1 smoked rainbow trout
   (approximately 200 g (7 oz) flesh)
2 long red chillies, seeded and
   finely sliced
1 large handful of mint leaves, torn
3 kaffir lime leaves, finely sliced
1 large handful of coriander
   (cilantro) leaves
125 g (4½ oz/½ cup) good-quality
   chilli jam
4 tablespoons crispy shallots
   (see page 42)
50 g (1¾ oz) salmon or trout roe

NAM JIM
4 red Asian shallots, chopped
2 red bird's eye chillies
2 garlic cloves, peeled
1 teaspoon chopped coriander
   (cilantro) root
100 ml (3½ fl oz) lime juice
75 g (2¾ oz) grated palm sugar
   (jaggery) (optional)
50 ml (1½ fl oz) fish sauce

To make the nam jim dressing, pound the shallots, chillies, garlic and coriander root using a mortar and pestle and then add the lime juice. Season with the palm sugar (if using) and fish sauce for a balance of hot, sour, salty and sweet.

Heat the oil to 180°C (350°F) in a wok or deep saucepan. Drop a cube of bread into the oil. If it bubbles up and turns golden, the oil is ready. Separate the won tons and gently fry in batches for 1–2 minutes turning once until light golden. Drain on the kitchen paper and allow to cool.

Flake the smoked trout, making sure you remove any bones, and combine with the chilli, mint, kaffir lime leaves and coriander leaves. Dress with some of the nam jim. Place a teaspoon of chilli jam on top of the fried won ton wrappers, place a small mound of the fish salad on top, sprinkle with the crispy shallots and top with the salmon roe.

This is such a simple recipe to prepare and very rewarding as your guests will think you have been slaving all day to create it. I have to say it is a real favourite of mine when catering for an event. Make sure you use beautiful, freshly cooked crabmeat (you can buy crabmeat already cooked and ready to go from the fish markets). Mud, spanner, blue swimmer, sand, snow or king crab also work well, but I think mud crab is the best choice for this recipe.

mud crab tortellini aglio e olio

Mix the crabmeat, parsley, lemon zest and oil together and season with salt and cracked black pepper.

Place a small amount of filling in the centre of each gow gee wrapper, then use your finger to dab a small amount of water on the rim of the circle. Fold over into a half-moon shape and seal. Take the 2 corner points and twist around your fingers to shape the tortellini.

For the sauce, heat the oil with the garlic, chilli and anchovy and cook until just starting to change colour. Add the parsley and cook for 10 seconds to release the flavour. Add the anchovy oil and season with sea salt. Cook the tortellini in boiling, salted water until tender and then lift out with a slotted spoon. Toss the pasta in the aglio e olio sauce and serve immediately either on a Chinese spoon or small plates. Garnish with lemon zest, grated bottarga and parsley.

MAKES 20

20 gow gee wrappers

FILLING
150 g (5½ oz) cooked and picked mud crab
1 tablespoon chopped parsley
2 teaspoons grated lemon zest
3 teaspoons extra virgin olive oil

SAUCE
100 ml (3½ fl oz) extra virgin olive oil
3 garlic cloves, peeled and finely chopped
1 long red chilli, finely chopped
2 anchovy fillets, chopped
1 teaspoon chopped flat-leaf (Italian) parsley
dash of anchovy oil

1 tablespoon grated lemon zest
1 tablespoon grated bottarga (optional)
chopped parsley, to serve

I've catered for a lot of events in my time and you wouldn't believe how many compliments I've had on these little tarts. For that reason, I had to include them in this book. Mushrooms may not be as colourful or pretty as the other ingredients at the greengrocer's, but when they're roasted then blitzed up, their deep nutty flavours emerge and create a wonderfully intense filling. Spoon that into some beautiful puff pastry and ... well it's a no-brainer!

wild mushroom tarts with sea salt

MAKES 20

600 g (1 lb 5 oz) field mushrooms, sliced
2 tablespoons olive oil
1 teaspoon sea salt
1 teaspoon cracked black pepper
2 teaspoons porcini powder
1 teaspoon dijon mustard
1 tablespoon crème fraîche
3 free-range egg yolks
2 sheets of frozen puff pastry, thawed
truffle oil, for drizzling

Preheat the oven to 180°C (350°F/Gas 4).

Lay out the sliced mushrooms on a baking tray and drizzle with the oil. Bake in oven for 20 minutes or until golden. Place in a food processor and process until smooth, add the sea salt, pepper, porcini powder, dijon mustard, crème fraîche and egg yolks and process to combine.

To make the pastry cases, lay out the puff pastry sheets and prick with a fork. Cut out 20 circles with a 5.5 cm (2¼ inch) round cutter, then line greased mini muffin tin holes with the pastry.

Spoon or pipe the mix into the pastry and cook for 15 minutes or until the pastry is golden brown.

Remove the tarts from the tin, drizzle over the truffle oil and sprinkle with some extra sea salt.

Not many things in life make me happier than sitting at the sushi bar in a great Japanese restaurant where I can watch the chef preparing my meal. I become mesmerised watching them meticulously slice the fish. There's no excuse for eating badly-made sushi when it's so easy to prepare yourself.

pete's sushi & tempura shiitake

MAKES 48 PIECES

To make the sushi rice, cook the rice with 330 ml (11¼ fl oz/1⅓ cups) water following packet instructions.

Meanwhile, stir the sugar, salt and vinegar in a small saucepan over low heat until the sugar and salt dissolves.

Spread the hot, cooked rice on a large tray and sprinkle over the rice vinegar dressing. Stir with chopsticks or a fork to cool and distribute the dressing evenly (see note). Press the rice into 24 blocks, each about 5 cm (2 inches) long and 2 cm (¾ inch) wide. Cover the rice with a damp cloth as you work.

Spread 16 of the rice blocks with wasabi. Place a wire rack over a naked flame and once hot, lay the salmon and kingfish on the rack until it gets lightly charred marks but is still raw. Cook on one side only. Place the raw side of the fish pieces down on the rice blocks. Squeeze some lemon juice over the fish and season with a little sea salt.

To make the cuttlefish sushi, top the remaining 8 rice blocks with the lemon zest and shiso. Score the top side of the cuttlefish with a sharp knife, making shallow incisions lengthways. Lay the raw scored cuttlefish on the rice blocks. Sprinkle with the toasted sesame seeds, if using and a little sea salt. Serve with soy sauce if desired.

To make the tempura shiitake, put the flour in a mixing bowl and slowly whisk in the cold mineral water, until the batter is the consistency of pouring cream.

Heat the oil to 180°C (350°F) in a wok or deep saucepan. Test with one mushroom: if it turns golden, the oil is ready. Dip the mushrooms into the tempura batter and deep-fry in batches until golden and crispy. Drain on kitchen paper, cut in half with a sharp knife and season with sea salt and a squeeze of lemon juice.

NOTE: Sushi rice is best when not refrigerated and used within 2 hours of making. However, if you like, you could shape the rice into blocks, place in airtight containers and refrigerate for up to 12 hours, then bring back to room temperature for 1 hour before finishing.

SUSHI RICE

210 g (7½ oz/1 cup) sushi rice
2 tablespoons caster (superfine) sugar (optional)
1 teaspoon sea salt
2 tablespoons rice vinegar

SEARED BELLY

2 teaspoons wasabi paste
8 x 20 g (¾ oz) slices of salmon belly
8 x 20 g (¾ oz) slices of kingfish belly
juice of ½ lemon

CUTTLEFISH AND SHISO

zest of 1 lemon
8 torn shiso leaves or baby shiso leaves, plus extra to serve
8 x 20 g (¾ oz) pieces of cleaned cuttlefish
1 teaspoon of toasted mixed white and black sesame seeds (optional)
sea salt
soy sauce, to serve (optional)

TEMPURA SHIITAKE

200 g (7 oz) tempura flour
350 ml (12 fl oz) cold sparkling mineral water
coconut or olive oil, for deep-frying
12 shiitake mushrooms, stems trimmed
juice of 1 lemon

This is a special-occasion recipe for me; it is a classic that has stood the test of time and probably the one offal dish that most people like. There are a couple of different methods for making pâté or parfait. A pâté is when the livers are cooked in the pan and then blended and set with butter; a parfait is when raw ingredients are blended together and then cooked slowly in a tin in a water bath. I have opted for a pâté recipe, as I like to be able to check I'm not overcooking the livers and, even more importantly, because I love the intoxicating aroma that fills the kitchen when I cook them. You can serve pâté with any type of bread — fresh crusty chunks torn off the loaf, or toasted sourdough — but my all-time favourite is buttery warm, delicately toasted brioche that melts in the mouth.

duck liver pâté with toasted brioche

MAKES ENOUGH FOR 1 LOAF OF BREAD

PÂTÉ

50 g (1¾ oz) clarified butter, for frying the livers

500 g (1 lb 2 oz) duck livers (soaked in 200 ml/7 fl oz milk for 2 hours, then strained)

3 garlic cloves, peeled and finely chopped

2 French shallots, peeled and finely chopped

1½ tablespoons chopped thyme

60 ml (2 fl oz/¼ cup) brandy

60 ml (2 fl oz/¼ cup) port

60 ml (2 fl oz/¼ cup) Madeira

1½ tablespoons dijon mustard

325 g (11½ oz) butter, at room temperature

1 free-range egg yolk

BRIOCHE

500 g (1 lb 2 oz) strong baker's flour

2 teaspoons salt

1 tablespoon caster (superfine) sugar

7 large free-range eggs

22 g (¾ oz) fresh yeast

60 g (2 oz) butter, softened and diced

Melt some of the clarified butter in a frying pan over medium heat and fry the livers in batches until just rare (wipe out the pan between batches), remove from the pan.

Add the garlic, shallots and thyme to the pan and sauté until transparent, then add the alcohol and flame to reduce to a honey consistency. Transfer to a blender and purée until smooth. Add the livers and mustard and purée until smooth. Add the butter gradually and season with salt and pepper. Add the egg yolk and blend until smooth, then pass through a strainer. Spoon into ramekins or a large terrine mould lined with plastic wrap, and leave to set in the fridge for 4 hours, or overnight.

To make the brioche, put the flour, salt and sugar in a mixing bowl. Using an electric mixer with a dough hook attachment, start the mixer on low speed and add 6 eggs one at a time. Add the yeast and continue to mix for 2–3 minutes. Add the butter, a piece at a time, and continue mixing for another 8 minutes. The dough should be smooth and elastic. Put in a large oiled bowl, cover with plastic wrap and leave in the fridge overnight.

Knock back the dough on a lightly floured work surface. Divide into two portions, shape and place on oiled baking trays or in two greased loaf tins and leave to prove until doubled in size. Preheat the oven to 180°C (350°F/Gas 4). Beat the remaining egg then brush the loaves with egg and bake for 20–30 minutes, or until golden.

I love visiting a new restaurant and seeing something I haven't seen before. A little while ago I happened to visit Coda in the heart of Melbourne's CBD. The chef/owner Adam D'Sylva has created a menu that is unique, with each dish calling out to be eaten. Luckily the menu is made up of lots of bite-sized morsels and I managed to ingest pretty much the entire range in one sitting. This dish, however, was a real standout — wonderfully crisp betel leaves filled with moist prawn mousse and fried to perfection.

crispy prawn & tapioca betel leaf

MAKES 20

Using a mortar and pestle, pound the garlic, chilli and ginger to a smooth paste. Place the paste, prawn meat, oyster sauce, fish sauce, sugar (if using), kaffir lime leaves and coriander in a blender and blend until smooth.

Heat the oil to 180°C (350°F) in a wok or deep saucepan.

To make the tapioca batter, combine the flours in a bowl then gradually whisk in the soda water until it is a pouring consistency.

To make the dipping sauce, combine the light soy and rice vinegar. Place the betel leaves shiny side down, spoon 1 tablespoon of the prawn mixture onto each leaf and close by bringing the tip and bottom of the leaf together. Dust in tapioca flour and shake off any excess. Then dip the leaf in the tapioca batter and drain off the excess. (The batter may start to thicken as it stands so you can add a little more soda water as necessary.)

Use one of the leaves to test the oil: if it bubbles and turns golden, it is ready. Deep-fry in batches for 4 minutes until crispy and cooked through. Drain on kitchen paper, season with sea salt and serve with the soy vinegar dipping sauce.

6 garlic cloves, peeled and chopped
1 long red chilli, chopped
1 x 4 cm (1½ inch) piece of peeled ginger, chopped
300 g (10½ oz) raw prawn (shrimp) meat
30 ml (1 fl oz) oyster sauce
30 ml (1 fl oz) fish sauce
3 teaspoons caster (superfine) sugar (optional)
12 kaffir lime leaves, finely sliced
¾ cup coriander (cilantro) leaves
coconut or olive oil, for deep-frying
20 large betel leaves
tapioca flour, for dusting

TAPIOCA BATTER
100 g (3½ oz/⅔ cup) tapioca flour
100 g (3½ oz/⅔ cup) rice flour
ice-cold soda water

SOY VINEGAR DIPPING SAUCE
250 ml (9 fl oz/1 cup) light soy sauce
150 ml (5 fl oz) rice vinegar

One of the most famous salads in the world, and the first one I learned to make at culinary school, is the Caesar salad. I can't tell you how many ways I have made this over the years or how many different ways I've been presented with it while dining. When it comes to a party, you can't beat serving it in a tart-shaped crouton topped with a quail egg — you may have to pre-order your quail eggs from the butcher, otherwise just boil some normal eggs and chop them finely.

caesar salad tartlets with quail eggs

MAKES 20

20 slices white or wholemeal bread
100 ml (3½ fl oz) melted butter
5 quail eggs
white vinegar
6 bacon rashers, cut into thin slices
1 small cos (romaine) lettuce
100 g (3½ oz/1 cup) grated
  parmesan, plus extra to serve

CAESAR DRESSING
4 free-range egg yolks
1 small garlic clove, peeled and finely
  chopped
2 teaspoons dijon mustard
2 tablespoons lemon juice
2 tablespoons white wine vinegar
5 anchovies fillets, finely chopped
400 ml (14 fl oz) extra virgin olive oil

Preheat the oven to 160°C (315°F/Gas 2–3). Remove the crusts from the slices of bread. Using a rolling pin, roll out the bread slices to 5 mm (¼ inch) thick. Cut out circles using a 7 cm (2¾ inch) diameter round cutter, brush with some butter and press into greased mini-muffin tin holes to form a crouton tart. Place in the oven and bake for 5–10 minutes, or until they are golden.

To make the Caesar dressing, place the egg yolks, garlic, mustard, lemon juice, white wine vinegar and anchovy in a jug and with a hand-held blender, start blending. Add the oil slowly until creamy and season with salt and pepper.

Place the quail eggs in a saucepan, cover with cold water and add a splash of white vinegar. Bring them to the boil, then remove from the heat immediately. Cool the eggs under cold running water, then carefully peel and cut into quarters.

Fry the bacon in a large frying pan over high heat until crispy. Remove to a plate lined with kitchen paper to drain and cool.

Just before serving, finely shred the lettuce and dress with a small amount of the Caesar dressing. Add the parmesan then fill the tart shells to just below the top. Place a quail egg quarter on the top of each and finish with a sprinkle of bacon, sea salt, a drizzle of the Caesar dressing and some extra grated parmesan.

Squid and chorizo is a wonderful combination (think of the Spanish paella) and a great way of having surf and turf at your next party. This is a simple, lovely recipe that will get the tastebuds jumping. You could also substitute the squid for cuttlefish, scallops or any type of fish if you wish.

ancho-spiced squid & chorizo brocheta with chipotle aïoli

MAKES 20

Soak the bamboo skewers in water for 1 hour.

Remove the skin from the squid and take out the cartilage from the inside. Cut open the squid lengthways, score the inside surface of the squid and cut into rectangular pieces about 4 cm (1½ inches) long.

Thread the chorizo and squid onto the skewers, so the chorizo sits inside the piece of squid.

To make the aïoli, place the egg yolks in a mixing bowl (or you could use a food processor), add garlic and lemon juice and whisk to combine. Continue to whisk, slowly pouring in the oil until the aïoli is creamy. Season with salt and the chipotle chilli.

Heat the olive oil in a wok or deep saucepan to 180°C (350°F).

Mix together the tapioca flour and the spices and coat each skewer in the seasoned flour. To cook, carefully place the skewers a few at a time in the oil and cook for 2 minutes until crisp and golden. Drain on kitchen paper and serve with the aïoli.

NOTE: Ancho chilli is a large, dried poblano chilli. Dark purple to black in colour and mildly fruity in flavour with subtle coffee notes, it is used in traditional Mexican dishes. Chipotle chilli is a delicious smoked, dried jalapeño.

BROCHETA
300 g (10½ oz) small squid tubes
4 chorizo, sliced thinly on an angle
olive oil, for frying
400 g (14 oz) tapioca flour
2 tablespoons ground ancho chilli (see note)
1 tablespoon cracked black pepper
2 tablespoons paprika

AÏOLI
5 free-range egg yolks
1 garlic clove, peeled and crushed
juice of 3 lemons
300 ml (10½ fl oz) extra virgin olive oil
1 teaspoon ground chipotle chilli (see note)

Yuzu is a citrus fruit from Asia with a distinctive sharp taste that is perfectly matched to seafood. If you can't get your hands on the fruit, you can also buy it bottled from Japanese supermarkets. This is a classic Japanese dressing that works with just about any type of seafood you choose to chop, slice and serve raw. Some of my favourites are scampi, prawns (shrimp), scallops, any type of white-fleshed fish and also the fattier fish such as salmon, trout, mackerel and tuna. You could drizzle this dressing over a freshly-shucked oyster for an appetizer made in heaven.

snapper tartare with yuzu dressing

SERVES 4

250 g (9 oz) snapper fillet, skin off
    and pinboned
50 ml (1½ fl oz) yuzu juice
1¼ tablespoons soy sauce
½ teaspoon freshly cracked pepper
½ teaspoon finely grated garlic
6 tablespoons extra virgin olive oil
1 jalapeño chilli, finely diced, to serve
small shiso leaves or chopped
    coriander (cilantro) leaves, to serve

Dice the snapper into small 1 cm (½ inch) cubes and place in a chilled bowl.

To make the dressing, combine the yuzu juice, soy sauce, pepper, garlic and extra virgin olive oil in a jar and shake well.

Pour over the snapper and toss to coat.

Divide between small glasses or spoons and serve immediately with the jalapeño and shiso to garnish.

A few years ago, when I was travelling through Victoria's high country, I stopped in at a local cafe called Coldstream Brewery. I lucky enough to order the right things off the menu (don't you hate it when you order the wrong thing and your mate gets the meal you wish you had ordered?). Well, everything I ordered from head chef Scott Arthur was unreal. This is one of the dishes I tried — great food, mate!

pumpkin, sage & parmesan fritters

MAKES 20

To make the caramelised onion crème fraîche, sauté the onion in a frying pan over low–medium heat in a touch of oil until soft and caramelised. Add the balsamic vinegar then remove from the heat and cool completely. Combine with the crème fraîche and double cream and season with salt.

Cook the whole potato in a saucepan of cold salted water, simmer until just tender and then allow to cool slightly. Peel the potato while still warm and then coarsely grate.

Sweat the onion with a pinch of salt and a touch of oil in a pan over low heat until soft and translucent. Place in a bowl with the potato, pumpkin, chopped sage, parmesan, egg, sea salt, cornflour and olive oil and mix until combined. Refrigerate for 1 hour.

Heat some olive oil in a wok or deep saucepan to 150°C (300°F). Deep-fry the sage leaves in batches until crisp. Drain on kitchen paper. Cook the fritters in batches, spooning tablespoons of the mixture into the oil and cooking for 5–6 minutes until golden brown and crisp. Drain on kitchen paper and serve with the crisp sage and caramelised onion crème fraîche.

125 g (4½ oz) desiree potatoes
75 g (2½ oz) onion, peeled and thinly sliced
200 g (7 oz) raw grated pumpkin
3½ tablespoons finely chopped sage
35 g (1¼ oz) grated parmesan
1 free-range egg, lightly beaten
1 teaspoon sea salt
70 g (2½ oz) cornflour (cornstarch)
1 teaspoon olive oil
olive oil, for frying
1 small handful sage leaves

CARAMELISED ONION CRÈME FRAÎCHE

2 large brown onions, peeled and finely sliced
2 teaspoons balsamic vinegar
200 g (7 oz) crème fraîche
50 ml (1½ fl oz) double cream

These are really nice canapés to serve at a party; small, elegant and super tasty, which is exactly what you're after with bite-size portions. I really love the flavour combination in this dish: caramelised bitter endive simmered with orange juice and sugar, teamed with crisp puff pastry and scallops. Without doubt, scallops would have to be one of the finest ingredients to come from the ocean. These could also be served as a starter with a larger pastry case and four scallops instead, and with a watercress salad on top.

caramelised endive tarts with seared scallops

MAKES 24

4 heads of endive (witlof)
2 tablespoons butter
3 tablespoons soft brown sugar
3 tablespoons orange juice
2 sheets frozen puff pastry, thawed
1 free-range egg, lightly beaten
24 scallops
olive oil
2 tablespoons salmon caviar

Chop the endive into 2.5 cm (1 inch) thick pieces. Fry in the butter in a large frying pan until it softens a bit, then add some sugar to sweeten. Cook until caramelised, then add the orange juice and cook until all the liquid has evaporated. Season with salt and pepper, then remove from the heat and leave to cool. Preheat the oven to 200°C (400°F/Gas 6). Lightly grease a tin of 24 small tart or muffin holes.

Spoon endive into the bottom of each tart hole. Top with a circle of puff pastry the same size as the hole. Brush with egg and bake until golden.

Sear some scallops until golden in a touch of oil in a frying pan over medium–high heat. Flip over for 10 seconds and then remove from the heat.

Turn out the endive tarts onto a platter. Top each one with a seared scallop and a little salmon caviar.

The grand master of Chinese cuisine and hospitality in Australia is the very affable Gilbert Lau. Thirty years ago, he started what is often considered the best Chinese restaurant in Australia, The Flower Drum. He now has Lau's Family Kitchen in St Kilda. Gilbert was a regular customer of mine at The Pantry and he kindly passed on his famous, and simple, scallop won ton recipe to me a few years ago.

steamed scallop won tons

MAKES 20

Chop the prawns to a fine mince, place in a bowl with the salt, white pepper, sugar (if using), olive oil and potato flour and beat vigorously to a smooth, firm mixture. Add the scallop meat, Chinese broccoli, bamboo shoots and ginger and mix well. Chill the filling in the refrigerator for at least 30 minutes before wrapping.

Cut the four corners of the won ton wrapper, making 1.5 cm (⅝ inch) slits. Hold the wrapper in the palm of your left hand, place 2 teaspoons of filling in the centre of the wrapper, and wrap the sides up. The filling should be seen above the wrapper like a dim sim.

Flatten the bases slightly. Place the dumplings into a steamer basket and place over a wok of boiling water to steam for approximately 10 minutes.

Combine the light soy sauce and chilli in a bowl and serve with the won tons.

40 g (1½ oz) prawn (shrimp) meat
¼ teaspoon salt
¼ teaspoon ground white pepper
¼ teaspoon caster (superfine) sugar (optional)
⅛ teaspoon olive oil
1 teaspoon potato flour
200 g (7 oz) scallop meat without roe, finely diced
2 tablespoons finely diced Chinese broccoli (gai lan)
1½ tablespoons finely diced bamboo shoots
1 tablespoon finely chopped ginger
20 won ton wrappers
125 ml (4 fl oz/½ cup) light soy sauce
1 green chilli, thinly sliced

I absolutely love serving this dish but I have to be honest, it's one of the most challenging recipes in this book. The main component here is, of course, the braised pork, which is delicious by itself or with steamed brown rice and Asian vegetables for a more substantial meal. For a canapé or finger food option, these steamed buns are something fun to serve the pork on. The addition of the pickled cucumber really cuts through the richness of the pork and a touch of hot chilli sauce, fresh Asian herbs and some toasted sesame seeds make this dish a real standout. It's definitely worth the effort.

steamed pork buns

MAKES 18

BRAISED PORK
325 ml (11 fl oz) shaoxing
   rice wine
150 ml (5 fl oz) soy sauce
200 g (7 oz) caster (superfine) sugar
1 knob ginger, sliced
5 garlic cloves, bruised
3 spring onions (scallions),
   roughly chopped
3 star anise
400 g (14 oz) pork cheek (or you
   could use pork neck)

100 ml (3½ fl oz) rice vinegar
100 g (3½ oz) sugar
2 Lebanese (short) cucumbers, finely
   sliced into rounds
2 tablespoons hot chilli sauce
coriander (cilantro) leaves, to serve
4 long red chillies, seeded and
   finely sliced

PORK BUN BASE
3 teaspoons active dry yeast
300 g (10½ oz/2¼ cups) strong flour
55 g (2 oz/¼ cup) sugar
1½ tablespoons instant skim milk
   powder
2 teaspoons sea salt
¼ teaspoon baking powder
¼ teaspoon bicarbonate of soda
   (baking soda)
35 ml (1 fl oz) olive or coconut oil

To braise the pork, combine all the ingredients (except the pork) in a saucepan and bring to the boil. Add the pork cheek and allow it to boil again, then turn down to a simmer, cover the surface with baking paper and cook for 1–1½ hours, or until tender. Allow the pork to cool in the stock, then remove and shred the meat. Strain the liquid, reserving some of the masterstock to moisten the pork when reheating to serve.

To make the buns, combine the yeast and 170 ml (5½ fl oz/⅔ cup) warm water in the bowl of an electric mixer fitted with a dough hook. Add the flour, sugar, milk powder, sea salt, baking powder, bicarbonate of soda and start the mixer on medium speed. Add the oil and mix until the dough comes together. Reduce speed to low and continue to mix for 8–10 minutes. Remove the dough, place in a greased bowl, cover with a tea towel (dish towel) and allow to rest in a warm place for about an hour, or until the dough has doubled in size.

Bring the rice vinegar and sugar to the boil in a small saucepan. Allow to cool. An hour before serving, combine the sliced cucumber with the vinegar mixture and set aside.

Line bamboo steamer baskets with greased, non-stick baking paper. Knock the dough back and cut into 3 pieces. Roll each piece into a sausage shape and cut each into 6. Roll into balls on a lightly floured surface. Flatten with the palm of your hand and use a rolling pin to roll them into 6 cm (2½ inch) diameter discs. Steam in batches for 4–6 minutes, or until cooked through.

Meanwhile, reheat the pork in a small saucepan over low heat with some of the reserved masterstock. Assemble the canapé by spreading a thin layer of chilli sauce on each hot steamed bun, add the cucumber, top with the braised pork and finish with the coriander and chilli. Serve warm.

This is a wonderful way to use leftover risotto from the night before but if you are purpose-making these, you can put anything you like in the arancini (risotto balls) that takes your fancy. Basically, any type of risotto you love makes for a great arancini. The reason I love this one is that it is my favourite type of risotto to make at home — full of flavour and visually stunning. It gets even better when you make the arancini as the outside crust gives a great contrast to the soft creamy risotto, and serving lemon wedges on the side for squeezing over makes them even nicer to gobble down.

spinach & taleggio arancini

MAKES 20

Make a spinach purée by blanching the leaves for 10 seconds in boiling salted water. Drain and then squeeze out the excess liquid while still hot. Process in a blender with the butter until emulsified into a rich smooth purée.

Heat the stock in a saucepan over medium heat to just below simmering.

Heat the oil in a separate small heavy-based saucepan over medium-low heat and cook the garlic and onion until softened and translucent. Add the rice and cook for 30 seconds, stirring well to coat all the grains with the oil. Add the wine and cook out the alcohol for a further 30 seconds. Add the hot stock and stir. Turn down the heat and simmer for 15 minutes, stirring often, until just cooked.

Remove from the heat and fold through the spinach and parsley. Season with salt and pepper, then fold in the taleggio and parmesan cheese. Spread onto a tray and allow to cool.

Once the risotto is completely cool, roll 3 teaspoons of the mix into balls and place into the refrigerator for 10 minutes, or until firm .

Whisk the eggs in a bowl with 50 ml (1½ fl oz) of water to make an egg wash. Place some flour into one bowl and the breadcrumbs into another bowl.

Dust the rice balls with flour, dip them in the egg mix, then coat with the crumbs.

Heat the olive oil to 180°C (350°F) in a wok or deep frying pan. Drop a small piece of bread into the oil. If it bubbles up and turns golden, the oil is ready. Deep-fry the arancini in batches for 3 minutes, or until golden brown and crisp, drain on kitchen paper. Season with sea salt and serve with lemon wedges and aïoli, if desired.

1 bunch English spinach, washed and trimmed (picked weight of about 125 g/4½ oz)
150 g (5½ oz) unsalted butter, softened
200 ml (7 fl oz) vegetable stock or water
2 teaspoons olive oil
2 garlic cloves, peeled and finely chopped
½ small white onion, peeled and finely chopped
110 g (3¾ oz/½ cup) arborio rice
50 ml (1½ fl oz) white wine
3 tablespoons chopped flat-leaf (Italian) parsley
70 g (2½ oz) taleggio cheese, cut into 1 cm (¼ inch) cubes
2 tablespoons grated parmesan cheese
2 free-range eggs
plain (all-purpose) flour, for dusting
100 g (3½ oz/1 cup) dry breadcrumbs
olive oil, for deep-frying
lemon wedges and aïoli (see page 127), to serve (optional)

If you really want to impress your friends at your next dinner party, or if you simply feel like treating yourself to a lovely lunch, then you can't go past this little number. It will take you less than 10 minutes to put together. The most important part of this recipe is to use the best-quality bread, fish and olive oil that you can. You can try it with other raw seafood if you like but I really think tuna is the best.

tuna crostini

SERVES 4

½ a baguette, sliced on an angle about 2 cm (¾ inch) thick
80 ml (2½ fl oz/⅓ cup) extra virgin olive oil
400 g (14 oz) sushi-grade tuna, cut into 1 cm (½ inch) dice
3 tablespoons lemon-infused olive oil
3 tablespoons chilli oil or 1 tablespoon chilli flakes
½ bunch chervil, picked
2 long red chillies, thinly sliced

Preheat the oven to 170°C (325°F/Gas 3). Lay out the sliced bread on a baking tray and drizzle with the extra virgin olive oil. Place the tray in the oven and toast for 5–8 minutes until golden brown, then set aside to cool completely. Alternatively, if you prefer, you can cook the bread on a barbecue chargrill like I've done here.

Combine the diced tuna with the lemon oil and chilli oil or chilli flakes in a small bowl and stir well until the tuna is evenly coated. Season with salt and freshly ground black pepper. Gently mix in the chervil and the sliced chilli, then place a spoonful of tuna mixture evenly on each of the toasted crostini pieces and serve.

Finger food should be eye-catching, tasty and neat, and these little sandwiches are all of those things. They are cut into perfect little rounds with a biscuit cutter and filled with a lovely combination of creamy champagne leek and steamed scampi. Topping it all with black caviar is pure indulgence.

steamed scampi sandwiches

MAKES 8 SANDWICHES

To make the champagne creamed leek, put the olive oil and leek in a saucepan and cook over medium heat for 3–4 minutes until the leek is softened but not coloured. Add the champagne and cook until nearly evaporated, then add the cream and cook until reduced by half. Season with sea salt and white pepper.

Cook the scampi in a steamer or in barely simmering water for about 6 minutes until they are just cooked. Remove the meat from the shells and cut in half lengthways, then leave to cool in the fridge.

Lay 8 slices of the bread on your work surface and top with the other slices to make empty sandwiches. Use a 5 cm (2 inch) biscuit cutter to cut out the middle of the bread so you have neat little round sandwiches (chuck away the crusts). Now take the tops off all the sandwiches and spread them with 2 teaspoons of champagne creamed leek.

Toss the scampi with lemon-infused oil, salmon roe, chervil and some sea salt and cracked pepper and put two halves of scampi on each sandwich. Now put the tops back on your sandwiches (press them down firmly), place a small amount of black caviar on top and serve with a flourish.

CHAMPAGNE CREAMED LEEK
1 tablespoon olive oil
1 leek, white part only, thinly sliced
250 ml (9 fl oz/1 cup) champagne
170 ml (5½ fl oz/⅔ cup) pouring cream

8 whole scampi
16 slices of buttered white bread
1 tablespoon lemon-infused olive oil
1 tablespoon salmon roe
1 tablespoon chopped chervil leaves
2 teaspoons black caviar

Squid, calamari or cuttlefish is always a big seller on restaurant menus, especially when served as a starter and deep-fried to perfection. As a chef, you want the dishes you create to be unique, jump off the menu and become a hit with your customers. However, it is the unwritten law that the most common thing will always sell more than something someone is unfamiliar with. This recipe is one sure way to have the majority of people at your next party think you're amazing. I've never met anyone that doesn't like fried squid.

sichuan spiced crispy squid with mouth-numbing sauce

SERVES 4

500 g (1 lb 2 oz) squid tubes
75 g (2½ oz/½ cup) plain
   (all-purpose) or coconut flour
35 g (1¼ oz) rice flour
1 tablespoon sea salt, plus extra
   to serve
1 tablespoon roasted and ground
   sichuan pepper, plus extra to serve
1 tablespoon ground white pepper
2 free-range egg whites
coconut oil, for deep frying
lime wedges, to serve

MOUTH-NUMBING SAUCE
1 tablespoon roasted and ground
   sichuan pepper
juice of 4 limes

Remove the skin from the squid and take out the cartilage from the inside. Cut open the squid lengthways and then score the inside surface. Cut the squid into thin strips about 4 mm (¼ inch) thick.

To make the mouth-numbing sauce, combine the sichuan pepper and lime juice.

Combine the flours, salt, sichuan pepper and white pepper in a large bowl. Beat the egg whites and lightly coat the squid in the egg whites and then dust with the flour mixture. Shake off any excess flour.

Heat the olive oil to 185°C (350°F) in a large, deep saucepan or wok. Drop a small piece of bread into the oil. If it bubbles up and turns golden, the oil is ready. When hot, cook the squid in small batches (so the oil stays hot and the squid gets crunchy) briefly until light golden in colour. Drain on kitchen paper, season with extra sichuan pepper and salt and serve in paper cones with lime wedges and the mouth-numbing sauce.

Salt cod (baccala) is one ingredient we Aussies and Kiwis do have to import from overseas. There's no substitute for the flavour of salt cod, but you could also use any other firm white-fleshed fish instead of the blue-eye. There is a bit of work that goes into making these fritters, but I dare say they would have to be one of my all-time favourite snack foods (the kids love rolling them, too). The good news is that you can make lots in one batch and freeze them prior to crumbing.

salt cod fritters with preserved lemon aïoli

MAKES 30

To make the garlic confit, place the garlic cloves and olive oil in a saucepan over the lowest setting possible on your stovetop (use a simmer pad if necessary) and cook for 1 hour or until the garlic is soft. You do not want the oil boiling at any time, you want it just past warm as this ensures the garlic becomes beautiful and soft—plus, you shouldn't get bad garlic breath if you cook it this way. Remove from the heat and allow to cool.

When the salt cod has been soaked, cut it into cubes. Peel and boil the potatoes until soft, then put through a mouli or grater.

Heat the milk, orange zest, bay leaf, shallot and garlic in a pan and add the salt cod. Bring to a gentle simmer and poach the fish for 15–20 minutes until half cooked.

Add the blue-eye and cook for another 10–15 minutes, or until the salt cod starts to come off the bone and the blue-eye is cooked through. Lift the fish out of the milk and leave to cool. Remove the flesh from the bones (making sure no bones are left in).

Finely shred the salt cod and blue-eye and mix with the potato, garlic confit, parsley, lemon zest, mustard and some sea salt and white pepper. Roll into balls, using about 1 tablespoon of mixture for each, and dip in flour, then beaten egg and then breadcrumbs. Heat the oil in a deep-fat fryer or large pan to 180°C (350°F). Drop a cube of bread into the oil: if it bubbles up and turns golden, the oil is hot enough. Deep-fry the fritters until golden and heated through.

Mix the aïoli with the preserved lemon and serve with the fritters.

NOTE: The garlic confit (with the oil) will keep in a sealed sterilised jar in the fridge for up to 3 months. If you are short of time you could roast garlic instead: Preheat the oven to 180°C (350°F/Gas 4). Place whole garlic on a large piece of foil, drizzle with a little olive oil, and seal. Roast on a baking tray for 30–40 minutes or until tender. Cool slightly then squeeze the garlic from the skin.

GARLIC CONFIT
1 cup garlic cloves, peeled
250 ml (9 fl oz/1 cup) olive oil

250 g (9 oz/¼ side) salt cod, soaked
  in cold water for 48 hours (change
  the water every 24 hours)
750 g (1 lb 10 oz) potatoes
500 ml (17 fl oz/2 cups) milk
grated zest of ½ orange
1 dried bay leaf
1 French shallot, peeled and sliced
1 garlic clove, peeled but left whole
160–180 g (6 oz) blue-eye trevalla
2 tablespoons chopped flat-leaf
  (Italian) parsley
grated zest of 1 lemon
1 tablespoon dijon mustard
plain flour, for dusting
2 free-range eggs, lightly beaten with
  a splash of milk
120 g (4 oz/1½ cups) breadcrumbs
coconut or olive oil, for deep frying
½ cup aïoli, page 127
1 tablespoon finely chopped
  preserved lemon rind

from the sea

I've had a love affair with the ocean for as long as I can remember. You couldn't drag me out of it when I was a kid, and I'm still at my happiest with a fishing rod in my hands or a surfboard under my feet. Maybe that's where my appreciation for seafood comes from. All I know is that fish and shellfish have been a major part of my diet for a long time and I love them however they come: raw, seared, poached, steamed and occasionally deep-fried. Over the years I've created, and had the pleasure of eating, some truly spectacular fish dishes. It was nearly impossible to choose my favourites for this chapter, so don't worry if you don't get your fill of seafood here; you'll find more seafood recipes scattered through the other chapters.

Aah, the mighty barramundi... Fishermen dream of heading north to tackle this magnificent creature; I just dream of eating it. Large fish can sometimes become a touch dry so my favourite way to cook barra is either pan-roasting or steaming. It can stand up to some pretty strong flavours, so is a perfect fish for mixing with Asian ingredients. This recipe here has become one of my best-loved dishes to serve when I'm asked to cook for special events, and I always get great feedback on it. If you can't track down any barra, you could always use jewfish, pearl perch, coral trout, red emperor, snapper or lobster.

steamed barramundi with lime coconut sauce

SERVES 4

Preheat the oven to 180°C (350°F/Gas 4) and bake the whole sweet potatoes for 1½ hours, or until tender.

Meanwhile, to make the lime coconut sauce, heat a touch of coconut or extra virgin olive oil in a pan and sauté the ginger, garlic, chilli, coriander roots and stalks and lemongrass until just starting to colour (save the coriander tops to garnish). Tear one of the kaffir limes leaves, add to the pan with the coconut cream and simmer for 30 minutes. Stir in the palm sugar (if using), fish sauce and lime juice. Purée and then pass through a fine strainer to remove any lumps.

Pound the ginger in a mortar and pestle, then add 125 ml (4 fl oz/½ cup) of water, then leave to infuse for 20 minutes to make ginger juice. Strain before using.

Peel the skin off the baked potatoes and purée the flesh with the ginger juice, butter and a bit of sea salt and white pepper.

Make a cut in the skin of the fish and then steam over fragrant, almost simmering water (you can throw in any Asian aromatics you might have around, such as lemongrass, kaffir lime, lemon, star anise) for 10 minutes or until the fish is just cooked through. You can tell when it's cooked because the cut in the skin will turn white.

Gently reheat the lime coconut sauce, then pour into the middle of the plate, place a mound of warm sweet potato purée on top, sprinkle over the crispy shallots and then cover with the barramundi.

Top with a couple of lime segments. Julienne the remaining kaffir lime leaf and sprinkle over the fish with the coriander leaves or some baby herbs.

LIME COCONUT SAUCE
coconut or extra virgin olive oil
2 teaspoons finely chopped fresh ginger
2 garlic cloves, peeled and chopped
1 green bird's eye chilli, finely chopped
½ bunch coriander with roots and stalks, chopped
2 lemongrass stalks, white part only, finely chopped
2 kaffir lime leaves
440 ml (15½ fl oz) tin coconut cream
2 tablespoons palm sugar (jaggery) (optional)
1 tablespoon fish sauce
1½ tablespoons lime juice

800 g (1 lb 12 oz) sweet potatoes, unpeeled
1 tablespoon finely chopped fresh ginger
1 tablespoon butter
4 x 160–180 g (6 oz) barramundi fillets, skin on and pinboned
2 tablespoons crispy shallots, (page 42)

A lot of the country's finest restaurant menus have one thing in common at the moment — raw fish. Whether it is a tartare, carpaccio or slices of sashimi, I am always drawn to raw fish as a starter choice. I know it won't fill me up, so I can still enjoy the next course. To serve raw fish at home is a lot easier than you might think: the only prerequisite is a sharp knife and the best quality seafood you can get your hands on. When you visit the fish markets or your fishmonger, you'll see a section called 'sashimi-grade'. These are the best pieces of fish available that the fishmonger has trimmed into a skinless boneless fillet, perfect for slicing up into sashimi, dicing into tartare or rolling out into carpaccio. The most commonly available sashimi-grade fish are yellow- and blue-fin tuna, ocean trout, Atlantic or New Zealand king salmon and hiramasa kingfish (a farmed, increased-fat kingfish from South Australia). Other varieties I like are snapper, paper thin-sliced whiting, scallops, lobster and cuttlefish. So next time you're at the fish markets, give raw fish a go — team it with this dressing, and you could be eating at one of the country's finest restaurants in your own home.

sashimi with japanese soy dressing

SERVES 4

200 g (7 oz) sashimi-grade fish (tuna, ocean trout, atlantic salmon, kingfish, scallops or prawns)
wasabi, to taste
pickled ginger (if you like)

JAPANESE SOY DRESSING
2 tablespoons sake
3 tablespoons mirin
250 ml (9 fl oz/1 cup) dark soy sauce
3 tablespoons tamari (Japanese soy sauce)
10 g (¼ oz) dried bonito flakes
1 teaspoon extra virgin olive oil

To make the dressing, combine the sake and mirin in a saucepan over medium heat and burn off the alcohol. Add the dark soy sauce, tamari, dried bonito flakes and extra virgin olive oil, then transfer to a bowl and leave overnight in a cool, dark place.

Strain the liquid through muslin or cheesecloth and store in a cool, dark place.

Slice your fish with a very sharp knife and arrange on a platter with wasabi and pickled ginger. Serve with the dressing.

When you're looking for a no-nonsense dish that lets the fish do the talking, this recipe is a great go-to. With just a little help from a simple dressing of red wine vinegar, paper-thin slices of garlic and fresh parsley leaves you have an impressive main course. As a good mate of mine called Squid said, 'Pete, I think that could be the best fish dish I have ever eaten'. That is probably the best compliment I have ever received from him, as he considers himself to be a bit of a connoisseur when it comes to seafood. This same method would also work well with any plate-size fish such as snapper, bream, sole or John Dory. Enjoy!

whole flounder with a warm dressing of garlic, parsley & red wine vinegar

SERVES 4

Preheat your largest frying pan to medium. Scatter a large tray with the flour and season with salt and pepper. Make 6 incisions across the top of the fish on an angle. Lightly dust the fish in the seasoned flour and shake off any excess.

Grease the pan with a little of the olive oil. Place the fish, skin side down, in the pan and cook until golden and crisp, then turn over, cover and continue to cook for a further 4 minutes or until just cooked through. Heat the oil and garlic in a saucepan on the barbecue until the garlic is just starting to colour. Remove from the heat and add the parsley and red wine vinegar (be careful as it may spit) and season with sea salt and freshly ground black pepper. Place the fish on a serving plate and spoon over the dressing. Serve with a beautiful salad and some lemon wedges, if you like.

plain (all-purpose) flour, for dusting
4 x 400 g (14 oz) whole flounders, scaled and gutted
125 ml (4 fl oz/½ cup) extra virgin olive oil
4 garlic cloves, peeled and very thinly sliced
1 large handful of flat-leaf (Italian) parsley
3 tablespoons red wine vinegar
lemon wedges, to serve (optional)

The difference between shucking your own oyster and buying one already opened is huge, mainly because when you shuck your own, the oyster in your hand is still alive. When you open the shell, the oyster should be completely covered by a juice, and this juice is very tasty. When you buy oysters already shucked, generally they have been washed of grit and all the lovely juices have been washed away as well. There is definitely a technique to shucking oysters though, and it's important to know what you're doing before you start wielding your shucking knife. So next time you're at the fish markets, learn how it is done, or jump online and see an expert do it.

freshly shucked oysters with ruby grapefruit, mint & chilli

SERVES 4

1 ruby grapefruit
3 tablespoons red wine vinegar
1 tablespoon caster (superfine) sugar (optional)
8 tablespoons extra virgin olive oil
1 large handful of mint leaves, very thinly sliced
1 long red chilli, seeded and finely chopped
24 oysters, freshly shucked

Peel and segment the grapefruit and slice into small pieces. Set aside in a bowl, keeping any juices that run off.

Warm the vinegar in a small saucepan, then dissolve the sugar into it (if using) and season with salt and pepper. Remove from heat, whisk in the olive oil, add the grapefruit and allow to cool. Stir in the mint and chilli.

Top each oyster with a spoonful of dressing and serve over crushed ice.

Catching and cooking your own mud crab is one of life's great pleasures. This is my version of chilli crab or Singapore crab. It may not be truly authentic, but it tastes so good that I don't really care! You could also use any crab, prawns, lobster, marron, bugs, mussels, pipis or vongole.

chilli mud crab

SERVES 4

Put the mud crabs in the freezer for about two hours, or until they are dead. Remove the top shell by lifting the flap on the underside. Remove the gills (the spongy grey fingers) and any muck by rinsing very lightly and quickly under running water.

Using a cleaver, cut the crabs in half lengthways, then cut into three on each side. Crack the claws with the back of a knife or cleaver so they open a bit to let the sauce in.

Heat the oil in a large wok and cook the garlic, chilli, ginger and coriander root until fragrant. Add the crabs and toss for a minute until they change colour. Add the tomato sauce, chilli sauce, stock (or water), hoisin sauce, fish sauce, sugar and salt, stir well and bring to the boil. Cover and simmer for about 10 minutes. Add the spring onions, herbs and cherry tomatoes. Serve with steamed jasmine rice, crab crackers, crab pickers, finger bowls and bibs.

4 live mud crabs
125 ml (4 fl oz/½ cup) coconut or olive oil
8 garlic cloves, peeled and chopped
4 long red chillies, chopped
4 tablespoons julienned fresh ginger
2 tablespoons chopped coriander (cilantro) root
250 ml (9 fl oz/1 cup) tomato sauce (ketchup)
125 ml (4 fl oz/½ cup) sweet chilli sauce
375 ml (13 fl oz/1½ cups) chicken stock
125 ml (4 fl oz/½ cup) hoisin sauce
2 tablespoons fish sauce
2 teaspoons sea salt
1 handful of chopped spring onion (scallions), green part only
1 handful of mixed mint, Vietnamese mint and coriander (cilantro) leaves
1 punnet of cherry tomatoes, halved

What I love about this dish is that it's indulgent, but fresh at the same time. There is the lusciousness of the rich omega-3 laden salmon fillet, the subtleness of the pea purée and the heat from the freshly grated horseradish, all with a simple radish salad to enliven the palate between each bite. Another great thing about this dish is that you can have it on the table in about 20 minutes. You could substitute ocean trout, rainbow trout or kingfish for the salmon.

Salmon with pea purée & red radish salad

SERVES 4

4 x 160–180 g (5½–6 oz) salmon
    fillets, skin on, pinboned
2 tablespoons olive oil
20 g (¾ oz) fresh horseradish, peeled
    and grated, for garnish

PEA PURÉE
650 g (1 lb 7 oz/5 cups) frozen peas,

HONEY MUSTARD SAUCE
2 tablespoons dijon mustard
2 tablespoons organic honey
1 free-range egg yolk
juice of 2 lemons
80 ml (2½ fl oz/⅓ cup) extra virgin
    olive oil

RED RADISH SALAD
1 small handful of podded broad
    (fava) beans (if using frozen, thaw
    and remove the skins)
¼ bunch of red radishes, thinly sliced
¼ fennel bulb, thinly sliced
⅓ cup chervil, picked or micro
    parsley or watercress
3 tablespoons thinly sliced celery
    hearts (yellow centre ribs of the
    celery), leaves picked and stalks
    thinly sliced
juice of 1 lemon
2 tablespoons extra virgin olive oil

To make the honey mustard sauce, place the mustard, honey, egg yolk and lemon juice in a bowl, season with salt and freshly ground black pepper and whisk well. While still whisking, slowly add the oil until the mixture is pale in colour and is a pouring consistency.

To make the pea purée, place the thawed peas in a blender with 1 tablespoon of water. Blend until smooth, then season with salt and freshly ground black pepper to taste. Pass through a sieve to allow the purée to become a smooth consistency, then set to one side.

Lightly coat the fish with 1 tablespoon of oil and season with salt and freshly ground black pepper. Heat the remaining oil in a frying pan over medium–high heat and cook the fish, skin side down, for 1–2 minutes, or until the skin is golden, then flip the fish over and cook for a further 2 minutes, or until the fish is medium–rare.

Meanwhile, to make the salad, blanch the broad beans in boiling, salted water, then drain and place in iced water to cool down enough to remove the skins. Combine the peeled broad beans with the radish, fennel, chervil and celery heart in a bowl. Add the lemon juice and extra virgin olive oil, season with salt and freshly ground black pepper and toss well.

Spread 2 tablespoons of the pea purée onto each serving plate and add a little of the mustard sauce. Place the fish on top and serve with the red radish salad and a few pinches of the fresh horseradish.

There are few things I enjoy more than eating fish and chips while I watch the sun set. The best fish and chips I've ever had was up in Darwin where they used threadfin salmon. If you are ever up north and you get the opportunity to try some threadfin, do yourself a favour and tuck in. If you can't track down any threadfin, you can also use gummy shark (flake), flathead, ocean perch, barramundi or whiting.

beer battered threadfin salmon with harissa mayonnaise

SERVES 4

To make the batter, pour the beer into a mixing bowl and gradually stir in the flour until the batter has the consistency of thick cream. Add the ice cubes to keep it cool. Use within 5 minutes.

Heat the oil in a deep-fat fryer or large pan to 180°C (350°F). Drop a cube of bread into the oil: if it bubbles up and turns golden, it's ready. Season the fish with sea salt and cracked pepper. Dust the fish in seasoned flour and shake off the excess. Dip the fish in the batter and drain off the excess. Deep-fry the fish until golden. Drain on kitchen paper and season with salt.

Stir the harissa into the mayonnaise. Serve the fish with harissa mayonnaise and lemon wedges.

olive or coconut oil, for deep-frying
4 x 150 g (5½ oz) threadfin salmon
  fillets, skin off and pinboned
plain flour, seasoned with salt and
  pepper, for dusting
1 quantity beer batter (see below)
1½ teaspoons harissa (a Middle
  Eastern chilli condiment available
  from delis)
4 tablespoons mayonnaise
lemon wedges, to serve

BEER BATTER
375 ml (13 fl oz/1½ cups) ice-cold
  beer or apple cider
plain flour or coconut
10 ice cubes

I don't think you can get any simpler than this. School prawns (or 'schoolies') are available all year round from the river mouths and inshore fisheries of the east coast of Australia, with peak supply from October to April. They are usually available cooked because they have a shorter shelf life than king and tiger prawns, but you can find them uncooked and frozen at the seafood markets. They are rarely deveined, and are only sometimes separated into three grades — small, medium and large. Schoolies have a distinct taste that is sweeter than most other prawns. For me, they are some of the best-value prawns available. They have been popping up on menus a lot lately; I think because they make a great starter or bar snack... but why go to a restaurant when you can cook them up in a few minutes at home? Serve with a good-quality aïoli and sea salt, make sure the sun is shining and these prawns will look after the rest.

fried school prawns with aïoli

SERVES 4

500 g (1 lb 2 oz) raw school prawns (shrimp), peeled and deveined, leaving the tails intact
tapioca flour, for dusting (optional)
1 litre (35 fl oz/4 cups) coconut oil
a pinch of chilli flakes
2 tablespoons chopped parsley
1 lemon, cut into quarters

AÏOLI
4 free-range egg yolks
2 teaspoons dijon mustard
2 tablespoons white wine vinegar
2 tablespoons lemon juice
6 garlic cloves, roasted, flesh finely chopped
200 ml (7 fl oz) olive oil
200 ml (7 fl oz) extra virgin olive oil

To make the aïoli, blend the egg yolks, mustard, vinegar, lemon juice, garlic and some sea salt with a hand blender. As you blend, slowly pour in the oil until the aïoli is creamy. Season with salt and pepper.

Coat the prawns with the flour if you like and shake off any excess. Heat the oil in a deep fryer to 185°C (350°F). Drop a cube of bread into the oil. If it bubbles and turns golden, the oil is ready. Cook the prawns in batches for about 1–2 minutes, or until golden and crisp. Drain on kitchen paper and transfer to a bowl.

Add the chilli flakes, parsley and some sea salt and gently toss. Arrange on a serving plate with the lemon wedges and some of the aïoli for dipping (the rest of the aïoli can be stored in the fridge in a sealed sterilised jar, as you would store mayonnaise).

Sardinians have a wonderful relationship with the ocean and it shows with dishes such as this. Which really makes the most of surf clams (or vongole, as the Italians call them). The use of fregola lifts this dish from one dimension into something beautiful that is just made for sharing with friends and family. Fregola is a Sardinian pasta, that is the size of a match head and very hard. It expands when cooked to look rather like large couscous and takes on the flavour of the sauce. Serve this with some crusty bread and a leaf salad for a great lunch.

vongole with fregola

SERVES 4

Gently heat the oil, garlic, onion and chilli in a large saucepan until starting to colour. Stir in the clams and then the fregola.

Add the tomatoes, basil and fish stock and cook over low heat until the clams open and the fregola is tender. Season to taste with sea salt and cracked pepper and add the lemon zest. Add the butter and leave to rest for 5 minutes before serving.

125 ml (4 fl oz/½ cup) extra virgin olive oil
3 garlic cloves, peeled and finely chopped
2 tablespoons chopped onion
1 long red chilli, finely chopped
800 g (1 lb 12 oz) surf clams (vongole)
40 g (1½ oz) fregola
625 g (1 lb 6 oz/2½ cups) tinned tomatoes, crushed
12 basil leaves, torn
310 ml (11 fl oz/1¼ cups) fish stock or water
zest of ½ lemon
1–2 tablespoons butter

There is a bloke who goes by the name of John Susman and if you ever get the chance to meet him or, better still, have a beer with him, he will talk to you about seafood like no other man can (Rick Stein excluded, of course). When he cooks a piece of fish, you sit up and take notice. This recipe is from the Susman family barbecue — it's an amazing dish and well worth trying at your next barbecue. If you can, look for hiramasa kingfish from the waters off South Australia as it has more fat than the regular kingfish. This, of course, makes it taste better, but also makes it more forgiving when cooking it on the barbecue, which is a beautiful way to prepare it.

Mr Susman recommends cutting the kingfish on an angle and cooking it right through. I don't mind it cooked to medium — I will leave that up to you.

hiramasa kingfish with hoisin glaze

SERVES 4

2 tablespoons olive oil
2 teaspoons sesame oil
4 x 160 g (5¾ oz) skinless hiramasa
    kingfish steaks, pinboned, cut on
    the angle
steamed jasmine rice, to serve

HOISIN GLAZE
4 tablespoons hoisin sauce
juice of 2 limes
1 tablespoon honey
2 garlic cloves, peeled and finely
    chopped
2 tablespoons chopped coriander
    (cilantro) leaves

To make the glaze, combine the hoisin, lime juice, honey, garlic, coriander, and some sea salt and pepper.

Mix together the olive and sesame oils and brush over the kingfish steaks. Leave to marinate for about 30 minutes.

Preheat the barbecue grill to high and brush with some of the oil marinade. Cook the fish on the hottest part of the grill, searing for about 1–1½ minutes, then turn over and cook for another 1 minute. Remove from the heat and cover the fish with foil to rest for a few minutes.

Drizzle the hoisin glaze over the fish and serve with steamed jasmine rice and an icy cold lager.

I was holding a cooking class for Tasting Australia in Adelaide (which has to be one of the best food festivals in Australia, hands down) and was intending to teach the students how to cook the best garlic prawns known to man. We had a little problem with the seafood for this event, so I went on the hunt in Adelaide to find some good fresh fish. I was advised to try Angelakis Brothers, and… let's just say that was great advice. Those guys know their seafood and have the very best of what South Australia has to offer. I ended up buying some sensational flathead and used it instead of the prawns — and the end result was as good, if not better, than what I'd been planning. The key to this story is to always use the freshest produce possible; if you can't find what you were hoping for, trust your instincts and you might just create a dish that's world class.

flathead with garlic, tomato & chunky bread

SERVES 4

In a cold saucepan, mix the oil, garlic, chilli and anchovies and then cook over medium heat until the garlic starts to turn golden. Use your spoon to gently break down the anchovies as they cook. Add the parsley and flathead and cook for 30 seconds on each side.

Add the tomatoes and water and season to taste. Simmer until the flathead is just cooked through and season with salt and pepper. Add the bread and let it soak up the oil before serving.

3 tablespoons olive oil
8 garlic cloves, peeled and thinly sliced
1 tablespoon finely chopped long red chilli
4 anchovy fillets
3 tablespoons chopped flat-leaf (Italian) parsley
400 g (14 oz) flathead fillets, skin off and pinboned, cut into large pieces
500 g (1 lb 2 oz/2 cups) tinned tomatoes, crushed
125 ml (4 fl oz/½ cup) sparkling or plain water
2 thick slices of ciabbata, toasted and torn in pieces

I know a lot of people say that you shouldn't do too much, or add too many strong flavours, to a piece of fish. I agreed in principle — that was until I tried this dish, which changed my mind entirely. Freshly chopped coconut with chillies, coriander, mint, turmeric and cumin made into a paste and smothered over a freshly caught fish and cooked either in foil or banana leaves really makes you glad to experience something new and exciting, that challenges your views and teaches you something new, like this did for me.

indian-spiced barbecue fish in banana leaves

SERVES 4

2 fresh banana leaves, centre
   veins removed (see note)
4 x 160 g (5¾ oz) pieces of coral
   trout or other white-fleshed fish,
   skin off and pinboned
lime wedges, to serve

COCONUT CRUMB
peeled flesh of 1 fresh coconut
   (about 375 g/13 oz), coarsely
   chopped (see note)
3 green chillies, coarsely chopped
1 large handful of coriander (cilantro)
3 large handfuls of mint leaves
125 ml (4 fl oz/½ cup) coconut oil
2 garlic cloves, peeled and crushed
½ teaspoon ground turmeric
1 teaspoon cumin seeds
juice of 2 limes

To make the coconut crumb, place the coconut, chilli, coriander, mint, oil, garlic, turmeric, cumin seeds, lime juice and some salt in a food processor and process until finely minced. Slowly pass each banana leaf over a medium-high flame until the leaf turns bright green. Alternatively, place the leaf on a barbecue hotplate and heat until it turns bright green, remove from heat and allow to cool.

Preheat the barbecue grill to medium. Place a fish piece on a banana leaf piece. Spread one-quarter of the coconut crumb over the fish. Wrap the leaf around the fish and tie with kitchen twine to secure. Repeat with the remaining ingredients.

Place the fish parcels on the barbecue and cook for about 4–8 minutes, or until the fish is cooked through. Serve with lime wedges.

NOTE: Heating banana leaves makes them malleable and easy to fold. If banana leaves are unavailable, use parchment (baking) paper or foil. Choose a coconut that feels heavy with no sign of dampness.

So many times in cooking, a food is really defined by the sauce with which it is served. The sauce is intended to enliven the palate and enhance the flavours of the food; it should never be overpowering. This recipe proves that a simple flavoursome sauce can really be a fish's best friend. I like to use coral trout or morwong for this dish, but you could use scallops, prawns, lobster, bugs, oysters, scampi, pipis, marron, crab or any firm white-fleshed fish.

steamed whole fish with shaoxing wine and soy

SERVES 4

Make three incisions through the skin into the flesh on both sides of each fish and then put the fish on a plate in a steamer. Mix together the rice wine and soy sauce and pour over the fish. Sprinkle the white julienned spring onion over the fish, cover and cook until the flesh is cooked through but still moist. Take the fish out of the steamer and serve it on the plate you cooked it on.

Meanwhile, heat the coconut oil in a saucepan and cook the garlic, banana chillies and ginger over medium–high heat until golden and crispy. Remove and drain on kitchen paper.

Drizzle the chilli sauce over the fish, if using, top with the coriander and green spring onions, scatter with the crispy garlic, chilli and ginger and serve with lime wedges, steamed rice and Asian greens.

2 whole fish (about 800 g/1 lb 12 oz each), scaled and gutted

125 ml (4 fl oz/1/2 cup) Shaoxing rice wine

125 ml (4 fl oz/1/2 cup) light soy sauce

6 spring onions, julienned, keep the white and green parts separate (keep the green part in cold water in the fridge)

250–500 ml (9–17 fl oz/1–2 cups) coconut oil

4 garlic cloves, peeled and finely sliced

2 long red chillies, finely sliced

3 tablespoons julienned fresh ginger

4 tablespoons chilli sauce (optional)

a handful of coriander leaves

8 lime wedges

A few years ago, I had the good fortune to go mushroom picking in a town called Oberon, which is just past the majestic Blue Mountains, west of Sydney. We were collecting pine and slippery jack mushrooms in a pine forest. I was amazed at how many there were and that they were free. Talk about a great tourist attraction — forget truffle hunting in Italy (which I think is overrated). The mushrooms we picked were in our pan that afternoon in a variety of dishes including mushroom bruschetta, steak with mushroom sauce and this one: rainbow trout with pine mushrooms. I had just been fishing in the local river and scored two beautiful brown trout. Before picking any wild mushrooms, check with the local tourism board to make sure you have the correct information. Many are poisonous and can be fatal so it's important to be well-informed before you venture out.

barbecued trout with pine mushrooms, prosciutto & garlic

SERVES 4

125 g (4½ oz) butter
4 thyme sprigs
4 rainbow trout, scaled and gutted
20 very fine slices of prosciutto
4 tablespoons olive oil
500 g (1 lb 2 oz) pine mushrooms, cleaned and sliced
2 garlic cloves, peeled and sliced
250 ml (9 fl oz/1 cup) white wine
1 handful of parsley, finely chopped

Preheat the barbecue grill to medium. Using half the butter, place a knob of butter inside each trout, then add a thyme sprig and wrap 5 pieces of prosciutto around each fish. Brush with 1 tablespoon of oil.

Cook the fish on the grill for about 4 minutes on each side, then remove and keep warm.

Place a large frying pan on the barbecue, heat the remaining oil until smoking hot. Add the mushrooms and cook for 2–3 minutes, then add garlic and cook for another minute or so. Add the white wine and parsley and reduce the wine by half, then whisk in the remaining butter. Season with salt and pepper and serve with the trout.

If you have read my books you'll know that I have a bit of a thing for the Northern Territory. The fishing, the weather, the markets, the magnificent landscapes, the whole laid-back nature of the place — it's like there's Valium in the water up there. Each year I visit to go fishing for a few days. While there recently, my mate Steve Travia cooked me this laksa — well really he only added the seafood to it as the laksa base had already been made by his good friend, Ibu Amye, who has a small Asian restaurant in Darwin called Warung Bu Amye. She gives him a bucket of her homemade laksa paste to put his catch into. You can do the same thing whenever you make the paste; just make extra, freeze it, then take it away on your next fishing adventure. Any white fish, or even prawns and mussels, will be delicious with this.

amye's laksa

SERVES 4

Soak the noodles in a bowl of cold water for 30 minutes to soften.

Meanwhile, process the garlic, chilli, lemongrass, turmeric and lime leaves in a food processor or pound using a mortar and pestle.

Bring the coconut milk to the boil in a large heavy-based saucepan. When it starts to boil, add the blended spice paste, palm sugar (if using) and tamarind and stir well. Add the barramundi, bring back to the boil, then turn off the heat and let it sit for 5 minutes, or until the fish is just cooked through. Break the fish into large pieces.

Add the fish sauce, lime juice, cabbage and tofu. Turn the heat back on and cook for a further minute, then remove from the heat.

Drain then divide the noodles and fish among four bowls, spoon over the laksa and garnish with the bean sprouts, basil leaves and crispy fried shallots. Serve with lime halves, a handful of trimmed bean sprouts, crispy fried shallots (see page 42) and half a bunch of thai basil leaves.

250 g (9 oz) rice noodles of your choosing
3 x 440 ml (15¼ fl oz) tins coconut milk
2 tablespoons grated palm sugar (jaggery) (optional)
½ teaspoon tamarind concentrate
500 g (1 lb 2 oz) barramundi fillet or other firm white fish fillet, skin off and pinboned
50 ml (1½ fl oz) fish sauce
50 ml (1½ fl oz) lime juice
¼ Chinese cabbage (wong bok), finely shredded
300 g (10½ oz) firm tofu, diced into 2 cm (¾ inch) cubes

LAKSA PASTE
6 garlic cloves, peeled
200 g (7 oz) long red chillies, roughly chopped
2 lemongrass stems, white part only, thinly sliced
1 teaspoon ground turmeric
5 kaffir lime leaves, finely shredded

This is a fantastic way to present a whole side of salmon or trout and I promise it will make your next barbecue a standout. As you know with curries, you usually fry off the curry paste then cook out your coconut milk and spices and this takes a bit of time. Not so with this method — you just mix the paste with the coconut milk and other aromatics and spread it over the side of salmon. The curry mix really gets into the flesh of the salmon, imparting its delicious flavour. Serve this on the centre of the table with some steamed rice and Asian greens for a very impressive lunch or dinner.

easy barbecued salmon curry

SERVES 4

1 side of Altantic salmon, skin on and pinboned, about 750g (1 lb 10 oz)
1 tablespoon Thai red curry paste
125 ml (4 fl oz/½ cup) coconut cream
2 teaspoons grated palm sugar (jaggery) or soft brown sugar (optional)
2 tablespoons fish sauce
2 tablespoons finely chopped coriander (cilantro) root and stem
2 lemongrass stems (white part only), finely sliced
4 tablespoons olive oil
3 tablespoons crispy shallots (see page 42)
1 kaffir lime leaf, finely julienned
½ cup coarsely chopped coriander (cilantro), plus extra for garnish (optional)
lime wedges, to serve

Remove all bones from the salmon using pliers or tweezers, then cut into the flesh in a criss-cross pattern.

Combine the curry paste, coconut cream, palm sugar (if using), fish sauce, coriander, lemongrass and half the oil and mix well.

Rub the mixture evenly over the salmon and marinate for at least 20 minutes.

Preheat the barbecue hotplate to medium–high and grease with the remaining oil. Place the salmon on the hotplate, skin side down, cover and cook for about 10 minutes. Remove from the heat and cool slightly before serving. Top with fried shallots and kaffir lime strips and coriander and serve with lime wedges.

Once in a while a dish comes along that really excites me and this is one of them. It has what I call the 'complete package' and for me that package has to contain the following: texture, flavour, aroma, eye appeal, adventurousness, playfulness, originality and, most importantly, it must be healthy! Two boys named Clint Yudelman and Noah Rose taught me this dish and it has become one of my favourite meals to prepare at home. You can do it with just about any type of white-fleshed fish, and I have found that it also works wonderfully with butterflied prawns (shrimp).

harissa-crumbed fish with tabouleh & tahini sauce

Preheat the oven to 180°C (350°F/Gas 4). To make the tahini sauce, whisk all the ingredients together with a tablespoon of cold water in a small bowl.

To make the tabouleh, place the burghul in a bowl and pour in enough cold water to just cover it. Stand, covered with plastic wrap, until the water is absorbed. Using a fork, fluff it up with 1 tablespoon of olive oil and sea salt to taste. Add the tomato, herbs, almonds, preserved lemon and pomegranate seeds and mix well.

Combine the remaining 3 tablespoons of olive oil, lemon juice and pomegranate molasses and season with salt and freshly ground black pepper. Mix well until it forms a dressing then add this to the tabouleh and stir until it is lightly coated.

Combine the harissa and panko crumbs in a bowl.

Season the fish fillets with sea salt and freshly ground black pepper, then brush with a little oil. Place the fish, skin side down, in a non-stick frying pan over medium–high heat and cook for 2–3 minutes or until golden (it may be necessary to hold the fish down with a spatula so it does not curl up while cooking). Remove from the pan and place on a baking tray. Press the harissa crumb mix onto the skin side and bake for 6–8 minutes.

Serve the fish with the tahini sauce, tabouleh and a drizzling of pomegranate molasses. Garnish with micro herbs or a parsley sprig.

NOTE: This recipe also works well with red emperor, barramundi, kingfish, snapper or blue-eye trevalla fillets.

SERVES 4

TAHINI SAUCE
2 tablespoons tahini paste
1 tablespoon extra virgin olive oil
1 garlic clove, peeled and minced
juice of 1 lemon

TABOULEH
2 tablespoons burghul (bulgur wheat)
4 tablespoons olive oil
400 g (14 oz) heirloom tomatoes, finely diced
3 tablespoons coarsely chopped mint
3 tablespoons coarsely chopped flat-leaf (Italian) parsley
60 g (2¼ oz/½ cup) slivered almonds, toasted
1 tablespoon finely chopped preserved lemon skin
50 g (1¾ oz/⅓ cup) pomegranate seeds
juice of 1½ lemons
1 tablespoon pomegranate molasses

HARISSA-CRUMBED FISH
2 tablespoons harissa paste
90 g (3¼ oz/1½ cups) panko breadcrumbs
4 x 200 g (7 oz) middle-cut coral trout fillets, skin on and pinboned
pomegranate molasses, to serve
micro herbs or flat-leaf (Italian) parsley sprigs, to serve

Though squid is always a big seller in restaurants, I think it has yet to be fully embraced in Australia as a choice for home cooking. It is always the biggest seller on any restaurant's menu, especially when coated in flour, deep-fried and tossed with chilli salt or the like. When it comes to home cooking though, I think it gets overlooked — probably because it can look a bit daunting to someone who has never cleaned squid before. Not only is it easy to prepare, it's really easy to cook so there's no reason not to add it to your barbecue repertoire.

chilli-spiced barbecued squid with salsa

SERVES 4

300 g (10½ oz) squid, cleaned
2 tablespoons olive oil
1 teaspoon chilli flakes
1 tablespoon chopped coriander (cilantro) root and stem
1 garlic clove, peeled and minced
pinch of ground cumin
pinch of ground coriander
2 tablespoons extra virgin olive oil

DONNIE'S FAMOUS TOMATO SALSA

6 vine-ripened tomatoes, roughly chopped
1 small red onion, very finely chopped
1 handful of coriander (cilantro), finely chopped
1 garlic clove, peeled and finely chopped
1 bird's eye chilli, seeded and finely chopped
juice of 1 lime

To make the salsa, combine all ingredients in a bowl and season to taste with salt.

To clean the squid, separate the head from the body (or hood) and legs by pulling the two apart, then take off the outer skin on the body by putting your finger underneath its two wings and removing them (the skin will follow with the removal of the wings). Pull out the long cartilage from inside the body (it looks like a long clear plastic straw that has been crushed), then make one cut down the body with a sharp knife to open it out and remove any membrane by running your knife gently over the inside of the flesh. As for the tentacles, just cut them off below the eyes and discard the eyes. Remove the beak (mouth) by pushing into the centre of the tentacles – a hard ball will pop out. If you want to score the flesh of the hood to make it curl up, then lightly run your knife across the flesh in a zigzag pattern or just cut into strips.

Cut the squid into 5 cm (2 inch) pieces. Preheat the barbecue hotplate to high. Mix the olive oil, chilli, coriander, garlic, cumin, coriander and season with salt and pepper in a bowl. Toss with the squid, then place the squid onto the hotplate and cook for about 1 minute.

Mix Donnie's salsa with the olive oil and serve with the squid.

This is a dish I've cooked at least 50,000 times (I reckon I have nailed it now ... ha-ha). It's got a lot going for it — it is easy, impressive and moreish. It has a fair amount of butter so treat it as an occasional dish, perfect for a celebration. Make sure you buy the best possible crabmeat for this or simply substitute prawns (shrimp). If you prefer, you can make it with noodles instead of linguine, as it does have some Asian flavours.

blue swimmer crab linguine

SERVES 4

Heat the butter in a frying pan, then sauté the garlic, chilli and shallot. Add 2 tablespoons of chopped coriander root and stem and cook until golden. Add the fish sauce and cook for about 10 seconds to release the flavour. Add the stock and tomatoes and reduce until you have a sauce that is thick enough to coat the pasta.

Meanwhile, cook the linguine in a large saucepan of boiling salted water until al dente. Drain.

Toss the pasta with the sauce and add the cooked crabmeat and chopped coriander leaves. Serve in bowls and garnish with a few more coriander sprigs and a squeeze of lime, if you like.

NOTE: You don't need to add any salt to the sauce as the fish sauce is salty enough.

80 g (2¾ oz) butter
8 garlic cloves, peeled and sliced
2 bird's eye chillies, diced
6 French shallots, sliced
1 bunch of coriander (cilantro), root, stem and leaves chopped
100 ml (3½ fl oz) fish sauce
1 litre (35 fl oz/4 cups) vegetable stock, fish stock or water
24 cherry tomatoes, halved
500 g (1 lb 2 oz) linguine
320 g (11¼ oz) cooked blue swimmer crabmeat (or use other crabmeat)
lime wedges (optional)

The 'wow factor' is the best thing about cooking for friends and family and even yourself (actually, I always put myself at the top of the list when I'm deciding what to cook... selfish, I know, but if I'm cooking I want the best). And I don't mean dishes that require a degree to construct, or an internship at a 3-Michelin-star restaurant to put together; the wow factor is simply how good the food tastes and how easy it is to make that happen. That is what I strive for in my home cooking: simplicity with great flavour. This dish does all that and more — it really lets the fish speak for itself with just an added chorus from some great supporting ingredients. You can use any whole fish for this (just remember to cook it for 15 minutes per kilo), but I love the flavour of ocean trout or Atlantic salmon. it just melts in your mouth and those omega-3s are an added bonus.

whole roasted ocean trout with lemon & herbs

SERVES 4

3 kg (6 lb 12 oz) whole ocean trout, scaled and gutted
1 small bunch of thyme
1 small bunch of oregano
1 lemon, halved and thickly sliced
8 garlic cloves, halved
1½ tablespoons olive oil

Preheat the oven to 190°C (375°F/Gas 5). Line a large baking tray with baking paper and scatter one third of the thyme, oregano, lemon and garlic across it diagonally.

Place the fish on top of the herbs and lemon and fill its cavity with the remaining herbs, lemon and garlic. Season well with salt and pepper. Drizzle the fish with the olive oil and roast for 45 minutes.

Check the fish is cooked by inserting a metal skewer into the thickest part of it. Hold the skewer there for 10 seconds and when you pull it out, check that the skewer is hot by touching it to the inside of your wrist. If the skewer is hot, then the fish is cooked. If it is only warm, the fish should be cooked for another 10–15 minutes before re-checking.

Serve the fish with a beautiful potato, egg and watercress salad.

This recipe is from Massimo Mele, a good mate of mine. His nonna used to cook this for him during summertime when he was a little kid on the Amalfi Coast. It's easy to make and absolutely delicious. Many people are put off by the thought of cooking octopus, but it really is one of the simplest seafoods to cook. This is a slightly unique way, as you are blanching it a few times before slow-cooking it. But it itsn't hard, and it's definitely worth the small effort required.

nonna's boiled octopus with potato, garlic, chilli & olive oil

SERVES 6

Place a large saucepan of sea water over high heat and bring to the boil. If sea water is unattainable, add 730 g (1 lb 10 oz/2 cups) of rock salt to 5 litres (20 cups) of water and bring to the boil.

Blanch the octopus three times in boiling water for about 5 seconds each time. Once complete, turn the heat down and add the octopus and potatoes to the same pan. Gently simmer for about 45 minutes, or until tender. Remove the octopus from the pan and set aside. If the potatoes need longer, cook them until they are tender. Let the potatoes cool down in the salty water.

Once the octopus is cool enough to handle, chop it into 5 cm (2 inch) pieces and put in a non-reactive bowl.

Peel and slice the potato into discs, add to the bowl with the octopus, then add all the remaining ingredients. Leave to marinate for 48 hours in the refrigerator.

Remove the garlic. Season with more vinegar and season with freshly ground black pepper. It shouldn't need any salt.

1 kg (2 lb 4 oz) octopus tentacles
3 large kipfler (fingerling) potatoes
5 garlic cloves, lightly smashed
1 long red chilli, sliced (seeds removed, if you prefer mild heat)
1 tablespoon chopped flat-leaf (Italian) parsley
1 tablespoon chopped marjoram
250 ml (9 fl oz/1 cup) white wine vinegar
250 ml (9 fl oz/1 cup) mild extra virgin olive oil
extra white wine vinegar, to serve

If you're in the mood for an impressive, hearty fish dinner, this one really delivers. I've cooked it for a few years now and the best tips I can give you are to make sure you buy beautiful fresh fish and use very good quality pesto. Ideally, I want you to make your own pesto. It's really easy, just whizz up a bunch of basil, a handful of pine nuts, a handful of grated parmesan and some extra virgin olive oil in a bender until smooth, then taste and correct the flavours with salt, pepper and maybe a squeeze of lemon juice. If you absolutely can't do that, hunt down freshly made pesto from a good deli. Get those two elements right and the rest will be easy.

kingfish with marinated eggplant & truffle sauce

SERVES 4

To make the basil oil, blanch the basil in boiling water and refresh in iced water. Strain the water off and wring out in a clean tea towel (dish cloth) to remove all moisture. Blend with oil in a blender and season to taste.

Take the top off both eggplants and cut them in half lengthways, then into three pieces. Season with salt, then place in a steamer over a pot of boiling water, cover and cook for about 15 minutes until soft.

Combine the dried oregano, olive oil, red wine vinegar in a non-metallic bowl. Add the the eggplant, leave to marinate for 5 minutes, then turn and set aside.

Place the potatoes in a saucepan with cold water and bring to the boil with a pinch of salt. Cook until tender then cool, then toss with a tablespoon of basil oil or pesto.

To make the truffle dressing, combine the balsamic, lemon juice and season with salt and pepper. Add the oils and egg yolk and whisk together until creamy.

Preheat the barbecue grill to medium-high heat. Season the kingfish with salt and pepper and brush with a little olive oil, then cook on the grill for a few minutes each side, or until cooked to medium.

Serve the kingfish on the basil potatoes and eggplant, with a drizzle of the truffle dressing and sprinkled with the chopped chives.

2 eggplants (aubergines)
10 g (¼ oz) dry oregano
100 ml (3½ fl oz) extra virgin olive oil
50 ml (1¾ fl oz) aged red wine vinegar
2 potatoes peeled and cut into 1 cm (¾ inch) cubes
1 tablespoon basil oil or good-quality pesto (see below)
4 x 200 g (7 oz) hiramasa kingfish cutlets or any other type of fish
3 tablespoons finely chopped chives

TRUFFLE DRESSING
50 ml (1¾ fl oz) white balsamic vinegar
1 teaspoon lemon juice
100 ml (3½ fl oz) extra virgin olive oil
2 teaspoons truffle oil
1 free-range egg yolk

BASIL OIL
1 handful basil leaves
125 ml (4 fl oz/½ cup) olive oil

This is the one of the nicest ways to eat a piece of fish cooked on the barbie. You do, however, need to prepare this dish a few days in advance as the fish needs time to cure in the miso paste, alcohol and sugar mix. Miso paste is made by fermenting rice, barley and/or soya beans with salt and it is used mainly in miso soup, which is made with the addition of dashi stock. It is a great flavour enhancer to meat or seafood when used as a marinade and it's also good for you, which is a bonus. But be careful as each paste varies from brand to brand and some are saltier than others. You can find this dish on many Japanese menus and it is usually cooked with cod, but I find coral trout, kingfish, salmon or ocean trout work a treat.

japanese miso-marinated fish

To make the paste, combine the miso, ginger, mirin, sake and sugar (if using), and stir until the sugar has dissolved. Place about a third of the paste on the bottom of a baking tray, then top with the salmon. Smear the rest of the paste over the salmon and leave, covered, in the fridge for 3 days to cure.

When ready to cook, preheat a barbecue hotplate or pan to medium–high. Take the fish out and wipe off all excess marinade with kitchen paper. Add a little oil to the hotplate or pan and cook for 4 minutes each side. Serve on a banana leaf with pickled ginger and garnish with the sliced spring onion.

SERVES 4

4 x 180 g (6½ oz) fillets Atlantic
  salmon fillet (skin on and pinboned)
2 spring onions (scallions), green part
  only, julienned
banana leaf, to serve (optional)
pickled ginger, to serve (optional)

PASTE

200 g (7 oz) white miso paste
  (saikyo miso)
6 slices ginger
1 tablespoon mirin
5 teaspoons sake
1½ tablespoons caster (superfine)
  sugar (optional)

If you love scallops as I do, this is such a quick and exciting way to prepare them. You don't need many ingredients, but the end result is so flavourful and memorable. Chipotle chillies are red jalapeños that have been smoked and dried, and they add amazing depth and heat to lots of Mexican and American recipes. You can buy them dried or in adobo sauce, which is basically a tomato sauce that's been seasoned and spiced. You can find both in plenty of good delis and food shops these days. Just go lightly with the chipotle even if you like a bit of heat. A little goes a long way, and you don't want to drown out the flavour of the scallops. What you're aiming for is an exciting contrast between the smoky heat of the sauce and the sweet delicate scallop meat.

scallops barbecued in the shell with chipotle chilli & coriander butter

SERVES 4 AS AN ENTREE

20 scallops on the half shell
200 g (9 oz) butter
1 large handful of coriander (cilantro) leaves, finely chopped
juice of 4 limes
2 garlic cloves, crushed
1 tablespoon chipotle chilli in adobo sauce

Preheat the barbecue hotplate to hot. To prepare the scallops, make sure they are free of any grit and the muscle on the side of the scallop is removed.

To make the topping, soften the butter then mix in the coriander, lime juice, garlic and chipotle chilli until well combined. Place 2 teaspoons of butter on each scallop and season with salt and pepper.

Place the shells on the hotplate and cook for 4–5 minutes with the lid down/closed so that the butter is sizzling and the scallops are just cooked.

Here's another recipe that really showcases squid in a wonderfully simple, but extremely flavoursome, way. If you can't buy the kang kong (water spinach), just use English or baby spinach. And don't be put off by the smell of the shrimp paste — you do need to use the amount it says, but it mellows during the cooking and becomes quite an integral part of the dish. Cuttlefish, prawns, bugs, any firm white fish and even salmon or trout are also delicious in place of the squid.

sautéed squid with malaysian water spinach

SERVES 4

Pound the garlic, chillies, macadamia nuts, shallots and shrimp paste with a mortar and pestle until you have a paste. Cut the stems off the water spinach and save them.

Heat the oil in a wok until it is smoking. Add the paste and cook for 30 seconds, add the squid and cook for 20 seconds, then add the water spinach stems and cook for 1 minute. Season with sea salt, add the water spinach leaves and cook until wilted. Squeeze some fresh lime juice over the top and serve.

4 garlic cloves
6 dried red chillies, soaked for 20 minutes in hot water, drained and chopped
4 macadamia nuts or candlenuts
5 red Asian shallots or French shallots
2 teaspoons dried shrimp paste (blachan)
300 g (10½ oz) water spinach ('kang kong' from Asian grocers) or English spinach
4 tablespoons coconut or olive oil
400 g (14 oz) squid tubes, cleaned and scored
lime wedges, to serve

I'm not sure we give the humble sardine the credit it deserves. We often think of it as a cheap, tinned fish. But, when bought fresh and cooked with just a few good ingredients, it really is one of the best fish you could eat in terms of flavour and cost. And in terms of the health benefits, well, where do I start? Sardines are one of the best sources of essential omega-3 fatty acids, which are fantastic for heart health. They are also packed with calcium — great for bones — and contain more than our recommended daily amount of vitamin B12, which our bodies use to produce healthy blood cells. Throw in lots of antioxidant properties and you've got a seriously super fish. Wrap them in vine leaves, like I've done here, or simply grill them until the skin is good and crispy. Your body will definitely thank you.

sardines in vine leaves with cherry tomatoes & olives

SERVES 4

1 bunch of oregano
12 fresh sardines, scaled and gutted
12 marinated vine leaves, rinsed
2 anchovy fillets
1 garlic clove, crushed
1 tablespoon finely sliced preserved lemon rind
1 handful of flat-leaf (Italian) parsley leaves, chopped
200 g (7 oz) cherry tomatoes, cut into halves
75 g (2½ oz) kalamata olives, pitted
juice of 2 lemons
150 ml (5 fl oz) extra virgin olive oil
olive oil, for cooking

Place a sprig of oregano inside each sardine and then wrap in a vine leaf. Season with salt and pepper.

To make the dressing, crush the anchovies in a bowl with a fork. Chop the remaining oregano and add to the anchovies along with the garlic, preserved lemon, parsley, tomatoes, olives, lemon juice and oil.

Brush the sardines with a little oil, then cook on a medium barbecue hotplate for 4 minutes on each side. Serve three sardines per person, topped with the dressing.

Ahhh, romesco sauce — I could eat it by the bucketload. It is such a good accompaniment but also so good by itself with some good-quality bread. It is a Spanish sauce made from roasted capsicums, hazelnuts, garlic, vinegar and olive oil — very easy to make and well worth it.

I have teamed it here with barbecued prawns in the shell as you always get more flavour in your prawns if you cook them still in the shell, as long as your friends and family don't mind peeling them; if they do, find new friends! It also works well with any piece of fish, chicken or lamb you decide to throw on the barbie.

prawns with spanish romesco sauce

SERVES 4

Preheat the barbecue grill to high. To make the romesco sauce, cook the capsicums on the grill, turning occasionally, for 15–20 minutes or until the skin turns black. Remove from the barbecue and let cool. Peel, deseed, discard the skin. Blend the capsicum flesh, garlic, hazelnuts, bread (if using) and vinegar in a food processor. With the motor running, add the olive oil slowly so the sauce thickens. Season with salt and pepper.

Cook the prawns on a barbecue hotplate preheated to medium for 2–3 minutes each side or until changed in colour and just cooked through. Serve with romesco sauce on the side and some fresh bread if you like.

NOTE: I've made the bread optional so if you are going for a thicker sauce (like the picture), include it. For a thinner sauce, that's more like a dressing, leave it out.

20 large raw prawns (shrimp), unpeeled

SPANISH ROMESCO SAUCE
3 red capsicums (peppers)
4 garlic cloves, peeled
150 g (5½ oz) hazelnuts, toasted and skins removed
1 sourdough bread roll, cut into 4 pieces (optional) (see note)
100 ml (3½ fl oz) sherry vinegar
300 ml (10½ fl oz) extra virgin olive oil

family feasts

Sitting down together as a family (with the TV off!) at the end of the day is non-negotiable at my house. I've heard people say that this is a dying tradition, but I hope it's not true. I can't think of anything better than sitting around as a family and talking over a home-cooked meal, and I like to think that my kids will feel the same when they grow up. This chapter is all about comforting, nourishing food that everyone — from Grandma to the youngest one — will love.

Some dishes, like the Italian meatballs or pot-roasted chicken with tarragon gravy, will be instant hits. Others, like the beautiful laksa or my Malaysian noodles, may be on the more adventurous side. That said, if anything feels too spicy or 'out there' for your kids, just tone it down by serving things like the fresh chilli and spicy sauces on the side.

There used to be a popular little Portuguese chicken burger shop around the corner from where I live. I would often pop in and order a burger after a surf. It consisted of a fresh burger bun lightly toasted with chicken fillets bashed out to within a millimetre of their lives and grilled with piri piri sauce and served with lettuce and mayo — utterly delicious and addictive. Since then, the little shop has gone and I have resorted to making my own... this is my recipe. It's pretty spicy — so be aware of that if you're cooking for kids. And please don't forget to wash your hands after handling those chillies. If you touch your eyes afterwards they'll be burning for ages.

barbecued piri piri chicken burgers

SERVES 4

To make the piri piri sauce, preheat a barbecue hotplate or chargrill pan to medium and cook the chillies for 5 minutes, turning occasionally until starting to blacken. Coarsely chop and place into a saucepan with garlic, 1 teaspoon sea salt, oregano, paprika, olive oil and vinegar and simmer for 3 minutes. Remove from heat and allow to cool, then process until smooth.

Marinate the chicken fillets in the olive oil and 2 tablespoons piri piri sauce for at least a few hours, if possible.

Preheat the barbecue grill to high. Scrape off the excess marinade and place the chicken on the grill. Cook for 2 minutes or until golden and marked on one side, then turn over and repeat until cooked through (if you need to cook longer, place on the barbecue hotplate to avoid excessive charring from the grill).

Butter the bread buns and grill lightly on the hotplate until lightly golden. Remove from heat and top the bread bases with the aïoli or mayonnaise, chicken, some piri piri sauce, lettuce and season with salt and pepper.

2 boneless, skinless, free-range chicken breasts, cut in half and bashed to flatten a bit
2 tablespoons olive oil
butter, for the buns
4 bread rolls or burger buns
60 g (2¼ oz/¼ cup) good-quality aïoli (see page 127) or mayonnaise
2 large handfuls of iceberg lettuce, torn

PIRI PIRI SAUCE
6–12 small red chillies, pricked all over
2 garlic cloves, peeled and coarsely chopped
½ teaspoon dried oregano
½ teaspoon paprika
100 ml (3½ fl oz) olive oil
50 ml (1½ fl oz) red wine vinegar

The Italians have a wonderful approach to cooking, which is why so many of their dishes become staples in our own homes even when we're not Italian! I remember reading a wonderful book called *The Food of Love* by Anthony Capella, who talks about food not only as a source of enjoyment but also as a means of transforming people's different emotional states. The dish I love to prepare, and the one which makes my daughters go crazy and chant 'more please, Daddy', would have to be Italian meatballs. The sheer simplicity of this is the key to its appeal, which will continue to grow as time goes by. You could add your favourite pasta to this, or better still, sandwich the tomatoey meatballs in a bread roll for a great lunch. It certainly transforms my emotional state.

italian meatballs

SERVES 4

350 g (12 oz) pork mince
150 g (5½ oz) veal mince
100 g (3½ oz) parmesan, grated
80 g (2¾ oz/1 cup) fresh breadcrumbs (optional)
2 tablespoons chopped parsley
2 free-range egg yolks
2 tablespoons olive oil
500 ml (17 fl oz/2 cups) Italian tomato sauce (see below)
shaved pecorino cheese, to serve

ITALIAN TOMATO SAUCE
2 tablespoons olive oil
50 g (1¾ oz) garlic, peeled and thinly sliced
500 g (1 lb 2 oz) tinned tomatoes, crushed
8 basil leaves

Preheat the oven to 180°C (350°F/Gas 4).

To make the tomato sauce, heat the oil in a saucepan and cook the garlic until it's starting to colour. Add the tomatoes and 125 ml (4 fl oz/½ cup) of water and simmer for 20–25 minutes. Add the basil and cook for another 5 minutes. Season to taste and blend until smooth.

Mix together the pork, veal, parmesan, breadcrumbs (if using), parsley, egg yolks and some salt and pepper. Roll the mixture into golf ball-sized balls.

Heat the oil in an ovenproof frying pan and fry the meatballs until golden on one side, then turn over and place in the oven for 5 minutes until cooked.

Add the tomato sauce to the pan and heat through on the stove top, then serve with the pecorino cheese.

Everyone has a handful of dishes that are firm family favourites and this is one of mine. There's nothing fancy about the recipe, it's just old-fashioned home cooking at its best. If your kids are fussy with vegetables, ask them to help you wash and prepare the vegetables before you start cooking. By the time they taste the finished soup they'll feel like they've had a part in making it, and the comforting bacony flavours should tip them over the edge. A big batch of this freezes really well, which is great for quick family dinners during a busy week.

vegetable & smoked hock comfort soup

SERVES 4

Heat the oil in a stockpot over low–medium heat, add the onion and garlic and cook gently until golden.

Add the ham hock, celery, parsnip, carrot, leek, corn, barley and soup mix to the pot with 4 litres (140 fl oz/16 cups) of water. Bring up to the boil, then reduce to a simmer and cook for 2 hours. Remove the ham hock from the pan and discard the fatty part. Chop the lean meat into pieces and return to the soup. Cook for a further hour.

Add the parsley and rosemary, then serve with a crusty bread roll or sourdough.

3 tablespoons olive oil
1 large brown onion, peeled and diced
3 garlic cloves, peeled and sliced
700 g (1 lb 9 oz) smoked ham hock
140 g (5 oz/1 cup) chopped celery (about 3 stalks)
130 g (4½ oz/1 cup) chopped parsnip
155 g (5½ oz/1 cup) chopped carrot
½ leek, white part only, sliced
200 g (7 oz/1 cup) fresh or tinned corn kernels
220 g (7¾ oz/1 cup) pearl barley
220 g (7¾ oz/1 cup) Italian-style soup mix (dried peas, lentils and beans)
1 bunch of flat-leaf (Italian) parsley, chopped
2 tablespoons chopped rosemary

I just had to include this classic. I can't think of anything better than to combine Australia's number one meat, lamb, with our favourite dish, the meat pie. To make a great meat pie you need to pick your cut of meat carefully — you want something that benefits from long, slow braising and in my opinion it has to be the shank. This pie does take some time to cook so plan well in advance and you can freeze any leftover filling for a smaller pie or tasty stew some other time.

Lamb Shank Pie

SERVES 4

4 lamb shanks, trimmed
2 tablespoons olive oil
3 carrots, chopped
3 brown onions, peeled and chopped
4 celery stalks, chopped
½ celeriac, cut into 3 cm (1¼ inch) chunks
2 large potatoes, diced
2 tablespoons plain (all-purpose) flour
400 g (14 oz) tin whole peeled tomatoes
550 ml (19 fl oz) good-quality red wine
100 g (3½ oz/⅔ cup) peas
⅓ cup chopped flat-leaf (Italian) parsley
375 g (13 oz) block of puff pastry
1 free-range egg, whisked with 1 tablespoon water

Season the lamb shanks with salt and pepper. Heat half the oil in a large saucepan or flameproof casserole dish over medium heat, then brown the lamb shanks on all sides until evenly browned. Transfer to a warm plate and drain off any excess oil.

Heat the remaining oil in the pan and add the carrot, onion, celery, celeriac and potato. Increase the heat to high and, as the vegetables begin to soften, reduce the heat to medium and cook for 15 minutes, stirring occasionally. Add half the flour and stir again so the vegetables are coated.

Meanwhile, put the tomatoes in a blender with the wine and remaining flour, then blitz until combined.

Add the tomato liquid to the pan and stir well. Return the shanks and any juices to the pan — it's fine if the bones stick out a bit but the meat section of the shank should be submerged. Add the peas. Place a lid on the pan and simmer gently for 2 hours over low heat. When the lamb shanks are cooked, lift them out of the pan with tongs, cool slightly and remove the meat from the bones, reserving the bones if you like. Shred the meat loosely and pour a small amount of the cooking liquor on top to keep it moist.

Return the pan to the stovetop, increase the heat and simmer the vegetables and sauce for 10–20 minutes, or until the sauce reduces. Remove from the heat, return the shank meat to the pan, add the parsley and season with salt and pepper. Set aside to cool. Preheat the oven to 180°C (350°F/Gas 4).

Transfer the mixture to a 2.5 litre (10 cup) ovenproof ceramic dish. Roll out the pastry on a lightly floured surface until about 3 mm (⅛ inch) thick and trim to the size of your dish, allowing an extra 3 cm (1¼ inches) all around. Place on top of the dish. Cut several slits in the top of the pastry for steam to escape while cooking and, if you like, carefully insert the bones through the slits. Turn the overlapping edges of the pastry under and crimp all around the casserole dish, ensuring the pastry is tightly secured. Brush lightly with the egg wash, then bake for 40 minutes, or until golden.

I spent a number of years of my apprenticeship working in Italian restaurants where I learned the finer details of making my own pasta and how to make the traditional pasta sauces. One of the most important lessons was learning how much sauce to pair with the pasta — a lot of people get it wrong and drown the pasta with sauce, when the sauce should only just coat the pasta and not overpower it. My favourite tomato-based pasta sauce is the classic amatriciana, a combination of pork, chilli, tomato, garlic and parsley tossed with bucatini, which is a thick type of hollow spaghetti. If you are cooking for more than six people I would suggest you swap the bucatini for penne, rigatoni or orechiette as they are easier pastas to toss through large quantities of sauce.

bucatini with chilli & pancetta

4 SERVES

Combine the oil, onion, garlic, chilli flakes and pancetta in a large frying pan and cook over low heat for about 12 minutes until the onion is soft and the pancetta has rendered much of its fat. Drain most of the fat out of the pan. Add the tomato sauce, turn up the heat and bring to the boil, then reduce the heat to a simmer and allow to bubble for 6–7 minutes.

Meanwhile, cook the bucatini in a large saucepan of boiling salted water until al dente. Drain.

Add the pasta and parsley to the simmering sauce and toss for about 1 minute to coat. Divide among four heated bowls and serve immediately, topped with freshly grated pecorino.

1 tablespoon olive oil
1 red onion, peeled, cut in half lengthways, then sliced into 5 mm (¼ inch) wide pieces
3 garlic cloves, peeled and sliced
1½ teaspoons chilli flakes
350 g (12 oz) thinly sliced pancetta or good-quality bacon
500 g (1 lb 2 oz/2 cups) ready-made tomato pasta sauce
500 g (1 lb 2 oz) dried bucatini
2 tablespoons finely shredded flat-leaf (Italian) parsley
freshly grated pecorino, to serve

This is a vegetarian dish I've been making for years. It was always popular on my menus and wasn't only ordered by the vegetarians presumably, as it was one of the best sellers. It's a dish that proves that good food doesn't have to cost an arm and a leg, or take hours to prepare. You can make this process even speedier if you buy oven-roasted tomatoes from the deli, and pre-rolled fresh lasagne sheets. Basil, tomato and cheese… it's a match made in Italian heaven.

tomato & ricotta tortellini with basil

SERVES 4

TOMATO AND RICOTTA FILLING
250 g (9 oz/1 cup) ricotta cheese
40 g (1½ oz/¼ cup) semi-dried
   tomatoes, finely chopped
1 free-range egg yolk
6 basil leaves, finely sliced
1 tablespoon grated parmesan
   cheese
1–2 tablespoons tomato juice (if you
   like)
1 tablespoon extra virgin olive oil

8 fresh lasagne sheets or 40 gow gee
   wrappers
1 free-range egg, lightly beaten
125 g (4½ oz) butter
1 tablespoon lemon juice
1 tablespoon extra virgin olive oil
8 basil leaves
8 red basil leaves
14 cherry tomatoes, halved and dried
   in a very low oven (or use fresh)
1 garlic clove, peeled and crushed
1 tablespoon grated parmesan
   cheese, plus some to serve

To make the filling, mix together all the ingredients. Place the lasagne sheets on a bench and cut into 9 cm (3½ inch) squares. Using a pastry brush, wet the edges of each square with beaten egg.

Place 1 tablespoon of filling in the centre of each pasta square and fold over diagonally to make a triangle. Brush a little more egg on two corners of each triangle and twist around your fingers so they come together. Press together to seal.

Cook the tortellini in boiling salted water for about 2 minutes or until cooked through, then lift out with a slotted spoon.

Heat the butter in a frying pan for 2–3 minutes until it turns nut brown. Remove from the heat and add the lemon juice and olive oil. Add the basil, cherry tomatoes, garlic, tortellini and parmesan and toss gently. Serve with some more parmesan over the top.

This dish is my version of a char kway teow which literally means fried flat noodles, which I have eaten many times in Malaysia at the markets and stalls over there. I do have to admit their version tastes slightly better than mine as they often cook it in pork fat and serve it with pork lard, which gives it its addictive flavour. I have opted for a slightly fresher version here using oil and the addition of some prawns, just because I love them.

malaysian noodles

SERVES 4

Place the noodles into a bowl and pour over some boiling water. Let stand for 5-10 minutes then gently separate the noodles with a fork. Drain and set aside.

Heat the oil in a wok over high heat. Add the garlic, ginger and chilli and cook for 1–2 minutes, or until fragrant. Toss in the sausage and spring onion and cook for a further 1 minute.

Add the prawns and stir-fry until just changing colour, then stir in the pork and cook for a further 2 minutes.

Combine the fish sauce and kecap manis and mix well. Pour into the wok and reduce until thick and sticky. Add the noodles, bean sprouts and chives and toss to coat. Serve immediately topped with peanuts.

NOTE: Sambal oelek is an Indonesian chilli paste, available from Asian food stores. If you are cooking for children, leave this, and the other chillies, out of the recipe. Serve on the side instead.

Lap cheong are dried Chinese pork sausages, usually smoked, seasoned and sweetened, available from the Asian section of larger supermarkets and Asian food stores.

Char sui pork is available from Chinese barbecue restaurants, which often have a shopfront for selling cooked meat.

500 g (1 lb 2 oz) fresh flat rice noodles
2 tablespoons coconut or olive oil
4 garlic cloves, chopped
2 cm (¾ inch) piece ginger, finely grated
2 teaspoons sambal oelek (see note) or 2 small red chillies, chopped
2 Chinese sausages (lap cheong sausages), sliced (see note)
4 spring onions (scallions), cut into 5 cm (2 inch) lengths
20 small raw prawns (shrimp), peeled and deveined, leaving tails intact
150 g (5½ oz) Chinese barbecued pork (char sui), cut into thin slices (see note)
2 tablespoons fish sauce
3 tablespoons kecap manis (sweet dark soy)
200 g (7 oz) bean sprouts
1 bunch garlic chives, cut into 3 cm (1¼ inch) lengths
40 g (1½ oz/¼ cup) roasted peanuts

If you are looking for a different way with roast chicken, then look no further. This one is cooked in a 'pot' with some beautiful ingredients that permeate the whole bird, and leave the meat wonderfully succulent. The glossy gravy that is made from the pan juices has tarragon leaves added and is really sublime. This is a very simple dish to cook, and I love to serve it with the cauliflower and taleggio on page 222, or with crisp croutons smothered with soft goat's cheese and flavoured with a hint of lemon and chilli.

pot-roasted chicken with tarragon gravy

SERVES 4

1 x 2 kg (5 lb) free-range or organic chicken
1 tablespoon butter
1 whole garlic bulb, halved
2 leeks, chopped into 3 cm (1¼ inch) pieces
2 carrots, chopped into 3 cm (1¼ inch) pieces
20 shiitake mushrooms (or other mushrooms if you like)
2 tablespoons olive oil
375 ml (13 fl oz/1½ cups) dry white wine
500 ml (17 fl oz/2 cups) hot chicken stock
leaves from 1 bunch of tarragon

Preheat the oven to 220°C (425°F/Gas 7). Turn the wings under the chicken and truss for roasting. Rub the chicken with the butter and garlic, then season.

Place the leeks, carrots, mushrooms and garlic in a casserole dish. Place the chicken on top of the vegetables, drizzle with olive oil and then pour the wine around the chicken (not over the top).

Roast for 30 minutes, then pour the hot chicken stock around the chicken. Reduce the oven to 180°C (350°F/Gas 4), cover with a lid and roast for another 30–45 minutes.

Lift out the chicken and vegetables (keep covered and warm) and strain the pan juices into a saucepan. Simmer over medium heat until reduced and thickened to make a glossy gravy. Add the tarragon leaves and check the seasoning just before serving with the chicken and vegetables.

This recipe is the result of my quest to find a crumbed dish — like a schnitzel, but not your ordinary schnitzel — for an unpretentious menu. After trying veal, chicken, fish and pork, I thought the pork cutlet was the winner. Adding parmesan and sage into the crumb mix took it from plain and simple to something with that little bit extra. This is a fantastic dish to cook at home or on the barbie and you can team it with a simple garden salad and lemon wedges, or try this elegant fennel salad.

parmesan & sage crusted pork cutlet with fennel salad

SERVES 4

Mix the breadcrumbs with the sage and parmesan. Season the flour with salt and pepper, then lightly dust the pork in the flour and shake off any excess. Dip into the beaten egg mix and drain off any excess, then place into the breadcrumb mix and press down firmly to coat the cutlet evenly.

Preheat a frying pan to low–medium. Add oil. Cook the pork for about 4–5 minutes on one side until golden, then turn over and cook for a further 4–5 minutes until golden and cooked through (you may need to pop into a warm oven for a few minutes to cook through).

To make the fennel salad, combine the fennel, parsley, olives, lemon segments, watercress, lemon olive oil and chives and place onto 4 serving plates. Top with the pork and serve immediately.

120 g (4¼ oz/2 cups) panko breadcrumbs or similar
1 handful of sage leaves, roughly chopped
35 g (1¼ oz/⅓ cup) grated parmesan cheese
plain (all-purpose) flour, for dusting
4 x 300 g (10½ oz) pork cutlets, trimmed
2 free-range eggs, whisked
olive oil, for cooking

FENNEL SALAD
1 large fennel bulb, shaved
1 large handful of flat-leaf (Italian) parsley leaves
10 green olives, pitted and sliced
2 lemons, segments only
1 large handful of watercress leaves
4 tablespoons lemon-infused extra virgin olive oil
20 g (¾ oz/⅓ cup) chives, cut into 3 cm lengths

This meal was served to me by my good mate, Nick Hannaford, who lives on Kangaroo Island in South Australia. Nick loves to entertain and show you the beauty of his home town, whether it be admiring the natural magnificence of the coastline while fishing from his boat or exploring the local food producers on the island. Nick is quite a natural in the kitchen and it shows with this simple dish. One thing I really love about it is that it tricks kids into trying artichokes, which can be helpful if you happen to have a fussy eater.

panko-crumbed fish with artichoke tartare

SERVES 4

ARTICHOKE TARTARE
2 free-range egg yolks
2 garlic cloves, peeled and chopped
4 small artichoke hearts from a jar
juice of 1 lemon
10 mint leaves, chopped
2 tablespoons salted capers, rinsed and drained
2 teaspoons fish sauce
100 ml (3 fl oz) extra virgin olive oil

75 g (2½ oz/½ cup) plain (all-purpose) flour
2 free-range eggs, lightly beaten
90 g (3¼ oz/1½ cups) panko breadcrumbs
700 g (1 lb 9 oz) flathead fillets or other white-fleshed fish, skin off and pinboned
185 ml (6 fl oz/¾ cup) coconut oil
lemon wedges, to serve

To make the tartare, place the egg yolks, garlic, artichoke hearts, lemon juice, mint, capers and fish sauce in a food processor, and blend. Slowly add the oil and keep mixing until it forms a thick consistency, then season with salt and freshly ground black pepper.

Place the flour in a shallow bowl, the egg in another and the panko crumbs in a third. Lightly season the fish with some sea salt, then lightly dust with the flour, coat in the egg then, lastly, firmly press on the panko crumbs.

Heat the oil in a frying pan over medium–high heat. Drop a cube of bread in the oil: if it bubbles and turns golden, the oil is ready. Fry the fish in batches for 30–45 seconds until golden and crispy, then turn over and cook for a further 30 seconds until crispy on that side.

Drain on kitchen paper to remove the excess oil. Serve with lemon wedges, a pinch of sea salt and artichoke tartare.

If you don't want to spend hundreds of dollars going out to the finest restaurant in town, why not whip up this little number? It might seem like quite a grown-up pizza (it is), but you might be surprised by what your kids will try if it's on a pizza. My girls loved caviar from an early age, so you never know. It has smoked salmon which is cheaper than valet parking, and you can either splurge on the best caviar or go for simple salmon roe (a less expensive type of caviar), which won't break the bank but will give you a wonderful flavour and texture. And the best bit? You can always get a table at home.

smoked salmon pizza with caviar & mascarpone

MAKES ONE 30 CM (12 INCH)
ROUND PIZZA / SERVES 1–2

Place a pizza stone in the oven. Preheat the oven to 180°C (350°F/ Gas 4). Cut the onion into 3 mm (1/8 inch) thick slices and toss in 1 tablespoon of the olive oil. Line a baking tray with baking paper and add the onion slices. Roast for 4 minutes or until the onion is soft.

Increase the oven temperature to 250°C (500°F/Gas 9) or to its highest temperature. Once it has reached the temperature, it will take about 15 minutes for the pizza stone to heat up.

Lightly dust a clean work surface with semolina or flour, then roll out the dough ball into a 30 cm (12 inch) round that is about 3 mm (⅛ inch) thick. Transfer the pizza base onto a piece of baking paper; this is necessary for transferring the assembled pizza to the heated pizza stone. Prick the pizza base all over with a fork or docker.

Spread the pizza sauce evenly over the pizza base. Sprinkle with the parsley and shredded mozzarella. Top with the onion. Transfer the pizza onto the heated pizza stone. Cook the pizza in the oven for 5–10 minutes or until golden and crisp.

Meanwhile, heat another tablespoon of the olive oil in a very small frying pan over medium–high heat and cook the capers until crisp. Drain on kitchen paper. To make the lemon dressing, combine the lemon juice and olive oil in a bowl and season with sea salt and freshly ground black pepper. Add the watercress and toss to combine.

Using a pizza paddle or wide spatula, carefully transfer the pizza to a chopping board or plate. Top with slices of salmon, the lemon dressing and dollops of mascarpone topped with caviar. Sprinkle with the crisp capers. Drizzle with the remaining teaspoon of olive oil and finish with a grind of black pepper.

½ red onion, peeled
2 tablespoons olive oil, plus
    1 teaspoon extra, to serve
semolina or plain (all-purpose flour),
    for dusting
170 g (6 oz) pizza dough ball
    (see pages 212–213)
60 ml (2 fl oz/¼ cup) pizza sauce
    (see page 213)
1 tablespoon chopped flat-leaf
    (Italian) parsley
50 g (1¾ oz) shredded mozzarella
    cheese
1 tablespoon capers, rinsed and
    drained
115 g (4 oz) smoked salmon slices
    (about 5 slices)
2 tablespoons mascarpone cheese
2 tablespoons avruga caviar

LEMON DRESSING
1 tablespoon lemon juice
1 tablespoon extra virgin olive oil
handful of fresh watercress

Now because the Italian word for sea is 'mare', a lot of people think a marinara pizza is a seafood pizza when in actual fact, it isn't; it is just a simple tomato, mozzarella, oregano and anchovy pizza. You can call the pizza below whatever you like, but it's definitely delicious. This pizza comes with all the trimmings. I like to include: mussels, clams, crayfish/lobster, shrimp, scallops, sea urchin, any of the fin fish and, of course, squid and octopus, in any combination.

seafood lover's pizza

SERVES 4

CHILLI CONFIT (MAKES 125 G (4½ OZ)
150 g (5½ oz) fresh long red chillies, halved, seeded and thinly sliced
125 ml (4 fl oz/½ cup) olive oil

10 black mussels, scrubbed and with beards removed
2 tablespoons white wine
160 g (5½ oz) raw medium prawns (shrimp), peeled and deveined, leaving tails intact
6 small scallops, cut in half lengthways
50 g (1¾ oz) baby octopus, cleaned, rinsed and halved
1 tablespoon finely chopped garlic confit (see page 108)
2 tablespoons chilli confit
1 teaspoon lemon zest
1 tablespoon olive oil
semolina or plain (all-purpose) flour, for dusting
170 g (6 oz) pizza dough ball (see pages 212–213)
80 ml (2½ fl oz/⅓ cup) pizza sauce (see page 213)
50 g (1¾ oz) buffalo mozzarella cheese, torn into pieces
1 tablespoon finely chopped flat-leaf (Italian) parsley, plus extra
2 lemons, to serve
2 tablespoons bottarga, finely grated (optional)

To make the chilli confit, place the chillies and olive oil in a small saucepan over the lowest heat possible on your stovetop (use a simmer pad if necessary). Cook for 1 hour or until the chilli is soft. You don't want the oil to boil. Remove from the heat and allow to cool.

Place a pizza stone in the oven and preheat the oven to 250°C (500°F/Gas 9) or its highest temperature. Once it has reached the temperature, it will take 15 minutes for the pizza stone to heat up.

Place the mussels in a saucepan with the white wine. Steam over high heat with the lid on for 2–3 minutes, or until the mussels open and are cooked. Discard any mussels that don't open. Remove from the heat and allow to cool before removing the meat from the shells.

Butterfly the prawns and place them in a bowl with the scallops, octopus, mussels, garlic confit, chilli confit, lemon zest and olive oil. Season with sea salt and freshly ground black pepper and leave to marinate for 10 minutes.

Lightly dust a clean work surface with semolina or flour, then roll out the dough ball into a 30 cm (12 inch) round that is about 3 mm (⅛ inch) thick. Transfer the pizza base onto a piece of baking paper; this is necessary for transferring the assembled pizza to the heated pizza stone. Prick the pizza base all over with a fork or docker.

Spread the pizza sauce over the base of the pizza and top with the buffalo mozzarella pieces, parsley and marinated seafood.

Transfer the pizza onto the heated pizza stone. Cook the pizza in the oven for 5–10 minutes or until golden and crisp.

Using a pizza paddle or wide spatula, carefully transfer the pizza to a chopping board or plate. Sprinkle with the extra parsley, add a good squeeze of lemon and the bottarga, if using, and serve with the lemon halves.

NOTE: Chilli confit (with the oil) will keep in a sealed sterilised jar in the fridge for up to 3 months.

One of my favourite recipes is steamed asparagus topped with a poached egg, nut brown butter sauce and truffled pecorino (it's on page 5 if you want to give it a try). I experimented with variations of this combination for quite a while before I came up with this pizza topping. It's fast become a favourite. When truffles are in season, shave generously!

asparagus pizza with goat's curd, egg & toasted walnuts

MAKES ONE 30 X 15 CM (12 X 6 INCH) OVAL PIZZA / SERVES 1–2

Place a pizza stone in the oven and preheat the oven to 250°C (500°F/ Gas 9) or to its highest temperature. Once it has reached the temperature, it will take about 15 minutes for the pizza stone to heat up.

Lightly dust a clean work surface with semolina or flour, then roll out the dough ball into a rough 30 x 15 cm (12 x 6 inch) oval that is about 3 mm (⅛ inch) thick. Transfer the pizza base onto a piece of baking paper; this is necessary for transferring the assembled pizza to the heated pizza stone. Prick the pizza base all over with a fork or docker.

Brush the pizza base with the olive oil and spread the goat's curd evenly over the top. Spread with the garlic confit, then add the shredded mozzarella, onion confit, parsley and asparagus, in that order. Season with sea salt and freshly ground black pepper.

Crack the egg into a cup. Transfer the pizza onto the heated pizza stone, then add the egg to the centre of the pizza and top with the grated parmesan. Season the egg with sea salt and freshly ground black pepper. Cook the pizza in the oven for 5–10 minutes or until golden and crisp.

Using a pizza paddle or wide spatula, carefully transfer the pizza to a chopping board or plate. Sprinkle over the shaved parmesan and the walnuts, drizzle with the truffle oil or shave over some fresh truffle and serve.

semolina or plain (all-purpose) flour, for dusting
170 g (6 oz) pizza dough ball (see pages 212–213)
1 tablespoon olive oil
60 g (2¼ oz/½ cup) goat's curd
1 crushed garlic confit clove (see page 108)
50 g (1¾ oz) shredded mozzarella cheese
1½ tablespoons onion confit (optional)
1 tablespoon chopped flat-leaf (Italian) parsley
6 asparagus spears, blanched and halved lengthways
sea salt and freshly ground black pepper
1 free-range egg
1 tablespoon finely grated parmesan, plus shaved parmesan, to serve
1 tablespoon toasted walnuts, crushed
1 teaspoon white truffle oil or fresh black truffle

There's a classic Italian dish called pasta puttanesca, which translated literally means 'whore's pasta'. There are a few stories as to where this pasta got its name, but all I know is that it's simple and delicious. The beauty of this pasta sauce is the combination of tomato, garlic, chilli, capers, olives and anchovies. All of these ingredients cry out to be placed on top of a pizza along with some creamy buffalo mozzarella.

puttanesca pizza

MAKES ONE 30 CM (12 INCH)
ROUND PIZZA / SERVES 1–2

semolina or plain (all-purpose) flour, for dusting
170 g (6 oz) pizza dough ball (see pages 212–213)
80 ml (2½ fl oz/⅓ cup) pizza sauce (see page 213)
1 tablespoon chopped flat-leaf (Italian) parsley, plus extra 1 tablespoon leaves, to serve
50 g (1¾ oz) shredded mozzarella cheese
12 cherry tomatoes, cut in half
1 tablespoon baby capers, rinsed and drained
6 pitted Sicilian olives, cut in half
1 crushed garlic confit clove (see page 108)
pinch of dried chilli flakes, to taste (optional)
sea salt and freshly ground black pepper
60 g (2¼ oz) buffalo mozzarella cheese, torn into pieces
6 white anchovies
extra virgin olive oil, for drizzling

Place a pizza stone in the oven and preheat the oven to 250°C (500°F/ Gas 9), or to its highest temperature. Once it has reached the temperature, it will take about 15 minutes for the pizza stone to heat up.

Lightly dust a clean work surface with semolina or flour, then roll out the dough ball into a 30 cm (12 inch) round that is about 3 mm (⅛ inch) thick. Transfer the pizza base onto a piece of baking paper; this is necessary for transferring the assembled pizza to the heated pizza stone. Prick the pizza base all over with a fork or docker.

Spread the pizza sauce evenly over the pizza base. Sprinkle with the chopped parsley, shredded mozzarella, cherry tomatoes, capers, olives, garlic confit and chilli flakes, if using. Season with sea salt and freshly ground black pepper.

Transfer the pizza onto the heated pizza stone. Cook the pizza in the oven for 5–10 minutes or until golden and crisp.

Using a pizza paddle or wide spatula, carefully transfer the pizza to a chopping board or plate. Sprinkle with the buffalo mozzarella pieces, parsley leaves and anchovies. Drizzle with some extra virgin olive oil and serve.

If you have read my barbecue book, *My Grill*, I hope you have come across (and cooked) the maple syrup and tamarind glazed pork ribs. If you loved that recipe, then I'm sure you'll also love this one. I remember Mum cooking ribs about once a month when I was a kid, and I always got super excited — I loved any excuse to eat with my fingers. and make a delicious mess.

mum's asian-style sticky pork spare ribs

SERVES 4

To make the marinade, combine the garlic, chilli, kecap manis, soy sauce, sugar, fish sauce, stock and star anise in a large saucepan and bring to the boil. Set aside and allow to cool.

Once the marinade has cooled, add the ribs to the pan, turning to coat them in the marinade. Cover and refrigerate for 2 hours or, for great results, marinate overnight if time permits.

Preheat the oven to 190°C (375°F/Gas 5). Place the ribs and any marinade in a baking dish, cover with foil or a lid and roast for 30 minutes. Remove the foil or lid, turn the ribs and baste with the marinade. Cook for a further 30 minutes, or until caramelised and lightly charred.

Sprinkle with sesame seeds and serve with jasmine rice and steamed Asian vegetables.

MARINADE
12 garlic cloves, peeled and minced
2 long red chillies, finely chopped
250 ml (9 fl oz/1 cup) kecap manis
250 ml (9 fl oz/1 cup) light soy sauce
185 g (6½ oz/1 cup) soft brown sugar
80 ml (2½ fl oz/⅓ cup) fish sauce
125 ml (4 fl oz/½ cup) chicken stock
8 star anise

2 kg (4 lb 8 oz) pork ribs, cut
   Chinese-style (ask your butcher)
sesame seeds, toasted, to serve

I thought I had tried every roast chicken recipe known to man; that was until I spent a few nights in Bali with local wild man Nicholas Morley. He and his friend, Ayu, prepared this chicken dish. I couldn't believe how easy it was to make, then in a few hours I was savouring every delicious mouthful.

balinese roasted chicken

SERVES 4

10 garlic cloves, peeled and finely chopped
6 long red chillies, finely chopped
1 knob of fresh ginger, finely chopped
1 small finger of turmeric, finely chopped
6 red Asian shallots, finely chopped
80 ml (2½ fl oz/⅓ cup) coconut oil
1 x 1.8 kg (4 lb) free-range or organic chicken
4 limes
10 fresh bay leaves

Combine the finely chopped garlic, chilli, ginger, turmeric and shallots in a small bowl. Heat a small frying pan with some of the oil, then fry off that aromatic garlicky paste over low heat until fragrant. Remove from the heat and set aside to cool.

When the paste has cooled, take a large sheet of foil and place the chicken in the centre. Slice the limes into quarters, then squeeze the juice over the chicken and rub the lime quarters into the skin. Wearing gloves, rub the cooled paste all over the skin of the chicken and inside the cavity. Place the lime quarters inside the chicken and season the entire chicken with salt and freshly ground black pepper. Lay the bay leaves on top of the chicken and wrap tightly in the foil. Leave to marinate in the refrigerator for a few hours or overnight if time permits.

Preheat the oven to 180°C (350°F/Gas 4). Keep the chicken wrapped in the foil, place it in a baking tray and bake for 1½–1¾ hours. Remove from the oven and allow to rest for 10 minutes before opening. Serve with rice.

This is a dish you can whip up in minutes, which is what I love about it. Just take an eye fillet, scotch fillet or sirloin — pretty much any nice cut — and bash it out with a rolling pin or meat tenderiser until it is about half a centimetre thickness all around. Pop it on a hot barbie or pan while you chop up the salad and you've got a beautiful meal in just a few minutes.

minute steak with green olive dressing & tomato salad

SERVES 4

To make the tomato salad, place the tomatoes, garlic, basil leaves, mineral water and olive oil into a bowl, season to taste with sea salt and cracked black pepper, then squeeze with your hand. Let sit for 10 minutes for the flavours to develop.

Preheat a grill pan and a frying pan to medium. To make the green olive dressing, sauté the onion with a little olive oil in the frying pan for a minute, then add them to a bowl with the olives, lemon juice, celery, olive oil, sea salt, pepper and chopped parsley.

Brush the steaks with a little oil and season, then cook in the hot grill pan for 1–2 minutes on each side, or until cooked to your liking.

Serve the steak topped with some of the olive dressing, and the tomato salad on the side.

4 x 150 g (5½ oz) sirloin or fillet steaks, bashed out
4 lemon wedges, to serve (optional)

TOMATO SALAD
30 cherry tomatoes, cut into quarters
2 garlic cloves, peeled and thinly sliced
10 basil leaves, torn
125 ml (4 fl oz/½ cup) sparkling mineral water
4 tablespoons extra virgin olive oil

GREEN OLIVE DRESSING
3 teaspoons finely chopped onion
125 ml (4 fl oz/½ cup) olive oil
110 g (3¾ oz/½ cup) roughly chopped green Sicilian olives
3 tablespoons lemon juice
½ celery stalk, finely chopped
3 tablespoons chopped parsley

Churrasco is a South American way of cooking meat, usually done on a rotisserie or spit. I have an amazing barbecue at home that has a couple of rotating electric 'swords' and I'm in the habit of throwing all types of meat, seafood and vegetables onto those swords and letting them cook over the coals and sawdust until they have a lovely smoky flavour. If you don't have a super-barbie, you can just as easily roast the beef or barbecue some steaks instead. The main drawcard here is the chimichurri sauce — it's a heady mix of chillies, herbs, vinegar, oil and spices and just about dances on your taste buds.

churrasco wagyu beef with chimichurri sauce

SERVES 4

CHIMICHURRI SAUCE
1 large handful of flat-leaf (Italian) parsley leaves
125 ml (4 fl oz/½ cup) olive oil
4 tablespoons red wine vinegar
1 small handful of coriander (cilantro) leaves
2 garlic cloves, peeled
¾ teaspoon dried red chilli flakes
½ teaspoon ground cumin
½ teaspoon salt

1 kg (2 lb 4 oz) side of sirloin or fillet of wagyu beef

To make the chimichurri sauce, blend the parsley, olive oil, vinegar, coriander, garlic, chilli, cumin and salt in a food processor. Pour over the beef, keeping about half a cupful of sauce to serve with the beef later. Cover then marinate in the fridge for 1–2 days, if you have time.

Take the beef out of the marinade and place on a rotisserie. Cook over an open flame for about 15–25 minutes, depending on how hot the flames are and how thick the meat is (you want to take the meat off the heat when it's rare and let it rest for 10 minutes before slicing).

Slice the beef and spoon the chimichurri sauce over it. Serve with some smoked tomato salsa.

This recipe is named for one of the nicest blokes I have ever met, Ian 'Herbie' Hemphill. Ian has a shop in Sydney called Herbie's Spices and from there he distributes his spices all around Australia. Cooking on a camp oven gives the dish so much flavour and it's great to make when away on holidays. However, if you want to make this at home, a large heavy casserole pan over a low heat for a similar amount of time will deliver equally delicious results.

camp oven lamb tagine by herbie

SERVES 4

Preheat the camp oven over medium–high heat. Coat the shanks with 3 tablespoons of the tagine mix, add oil to the camp oven and seal the shanks lightly in batches.

Return all the shanks to the camp oven. Add the parsnip, carrot, onion, prunes, remaining tagine mix, peppercorns, garlic, tomato paste, tomatoes, orange juice and 1 litre (35 fl oz/4 cups) of water. Cover with lid or foil and gently simmer for 1½–2 hours, or until the meat is very tender. Season with salt. Serve with couscous and chopped parsley.

NOTE: This tagine mix makes more than 4 tablespoons. Store the leftover mix in an airtight container for up to 1 month. Alternatively, you can buy tagine mix from gourmet food stores or Herbie's Spices.

8 small lamb shanks
4 tablespoons tagine mix (see note)
2 tablespoons olive oil
2 parsnips, peeled and cubed
4 carrots, chopped
3 onions, peeled and finely chopped
6 prunes, pitted
3–4 black peppercorns, crushed
8 garlic cloves, peeled and minced
2 tablespoons tomato paste
  (concentrated purée)
400 g (14 oz) tinned crushed
  tomatoes
500 ml (17 fl oz/2 cups) orange juice
freshly cooked couscous, to serve
chopped flat-leaf (Italian) parsley,
  to serve

TAGINE MIX
2½ tablespoons mild paprika
5 teaspoons ground coriander seeds
2 teaspoons ground cassia bark
2 teaspoons medium-heat
  dried chilli
1 teaspoon ground allspice
½ teaspoon ground cloves
½ teaspoon green cardamom seeds

One country I'd love to visit is Greece. It looks beautiful and I can't wait to visit its islands and eat octopus from their waters and lamb from their fields. But until that day, here's a simple little recipe that conjures up the beautiful Greek flavours that I love — zucchini, anchovies, garlic and feta, not to mention the lamb. I have used lamb chops here as I really do think it is a fantastic cut of meat to cook on the barbie. It is quick and super-tasty due to the fat (which you can easily remove once it has been cooked). It's also pretty hard to get it wrong when cooking chops.

greek-style lamb chops with zucchini salad & anchovy & feta dressing

SERVES 4

2 garlic cloves, peeled and finely chopped
6 tablespoons extra virgin olive oil
1 teaspoon dried Greek oregano (see note)
8 lamb loin chops
2 large zucchini (courgettes), cut into 5 mm (¼ inch) thick slices
3 anchovy fillets, torn into pieces
1 tablespoon pine nuts, toasted
80 g (2¾ oz) feta cheese, crumbled
pinch of chilli flakes
1 small handful of oregano leaves
juice of ½ lemon
40 g (1½ oz/¼ cup) Kalamata olives

Combine the garlic, 2 tablespoons of the oil and dried oregano in a bowl and season with sea salt and cracked black pepper. Use this mixture to marinate the lamb chops for at least 30 minutes.

Preheat the barbecue hotplate or grill to high. Cook the lamb for 2–3 minutes each side, or until cooked to your liking.

Coat the zucchini slices with oil and some sea salt and cracked black pepper and cook on the barbecue or in a hot pan until golden. Toss into a bowl with the anchovies, pine nuts, feta, chilli, remaining olive oil, fresh oregano, lemon juice and olives.

Serve the lamb chops with the warm zucchini salad.

NOTE: Dried Greek oregano is available from good delicatessens. If unavailable, use regular dried oregano.

Mmm, roast lamb… how good is it when you're going to someone's house for dinner and they tell you they're cooking roast lamb? Or, even better, when you come home from work, open the front door and smell lamb roasting in your own home? This is how I cook it when I want to spice things up a bit and hands down, I reckon it's one of the best lamb recipes I've ever written. Harissa is a North African spice paste made of chillies, garlic, cumin, coriander and olive oil and is very seductive when used sparingly — it is nice and spicy so it excites the palate and leaves you craving more. Here I have teamed the lamb with a very simple roast pumpkin salad and used a beautiful dressing made from pomegranate molasses. If you're partial to salads, this one is even great as the main on its own.

harissa lamb leg with roasted pumpkin, feta & pomegranate salad

SERVES 4

Bring the lamb leg to room temperature (and make sure you know how much it weighs). Preheat the oven to 180°C (350°F/Gas 4). Coat the lamb with the harissa paste, then with the olive oil.

Roast the lamb for 45 minutes, and then another 25 minutes per kilo of weight. Remove from the oven and turn the heat up to 200°C (400°F/Gas 6). Put the lamb aside and leave to rest, loosely covered with foil, for about 30 minutes.

Put the pumpkin and onion in a roasting tin and toss with the cumin, chilli flakes and some sea salt and pepper. Drizzle with the olive oil and roast until golden. Toss with the mint, feta and pine nuts. Drizzle with the pomegranate molasses and pomegranate seeds then slice up the lamb and serve.

1 lamb leg (2–3 kg/4 lb 8 oz–6 lb 12 oz), bone in
4 tablespoons harissa paste
1 tablespoon extra virgin olive oil

ROASTED PUMPKIN, FETA AND POMEGRANATE SALAD
600 g (1 lb 5 oz) pumpkin, unpeeled and chopped
1 small red onion, peeled and cut into wedges
a pinch of ground cumin
a pinch of chilli flakes
1 tablespoon extra virgin olive oil
1 handful of mint leaves
120 g (4 oz) sheep's milk feta (Persian is great)
2 tablespoons pine nuts, roasted
1–2 tablespoons pomegranate molasses
2 tablespoons pomegranate seeds

My Christmas day ritual is to get up early and go surfing. Chrissy day is one of the most uncrowded times in the waves as everyone is at home opening up their presents. Because of this early morning escape, and the fact that I'm always blessed with doing the cooking honours on the day, I like to make it all as painless and indulgent as possible. Hence my baked Christmas ham. This can be cooked a day in advance and it actually tastes better the next day. The recipe was handed to me by a very good friend of mine, Rob Vandyke, stepfather of Maddie Hayes, one of the best apprentices I've ever had. Sadly, Rob has passed away, but his memory will live on in our hearts and his superb ham will be forever on my Christmas table.

rob's christmas ham with fennel coleslaw

SERVES 4

Stir the apricot jam and sherry in a saucepan over medium heat until it becomes a sticky spread. Preheat the oven to 180°C (350°F/Gas 4). Prepare the ham by lifting off the skin but leaving the fat. Score the fat into diamonds about 2.5 cm (1 inch) deep. (This helps to open the ham up and get the flavour of the glaze into the meat.)

Mix the cinnamon with the star anise and rub into the fat. Spread two-thirds of the apricot glaze over the ham (keep the rest for basting). Press the brown sugar over the top, making sure some sugar gets into the score marks.

Put the ham in a roasting tin, add 2 cm (¾ inch) of water and cook for 1–1½ hours, basting with the remaining glaze from time to time. Be careful not to let the ham burn — check it every 20 minutes or so.

Once the ham is out of the oven, get started on the coleslaw. Combine all the ingredients in a large bowl. Gently toss together and check the seasoning.

Serve the ham with the fennel coleslaw, your favourite chutney, mustard and crusty bread.

500 g (1 lb 2 oz) apricot jam
185 ml (6 fl oz/¾ cup) dry sherry
1 large cooked cold leg of ham
1 tablespoon ground cinnamon
7 star anise, ground with a mortar
    and pestle
95 g (3½ oz/½ cup) soft brown sugar

FENNEL COLESLAW
¼ purple cabbage, cut into thin strips
¼ green cabbage, cut into thin strips
2 fennel bulbs, finely shaved
6 radishes, cut into thin rounds
2 long red chillies, deseeded and
    finely sliced
½ red onion, peeled and finely sliced
2 carrots, grated
juice of 1 lemon
4 tablespoons extra virgin olive oil
1 tablespoon seeded mustard
250 g (9 oz/1 cup) plain yoghurt
    or mayonnaise
2–3 large handfuls of herbs such
    as parsley, dill, basil, chives and
    tarragon, roughly chopped

The following dough recipes each make one large quantity of dough, which can then be split into separate portions. The recipes in this book call for 170 g (6 oz) balls of dough. You can substitute wholemeal (whole-wheat) or gluten-free dough for the classic dough in most recipes. (Please see note at the end of the gluten-free dough recipe for any restrictions.)

classic pizza dough

MAKES 750 G (1 LB 10 OZ) /
ROUGHLY ENOUGH FOR FOUR
30 CM (12 INCH) PIZZAS

250 ml (9 fl oz/1 cup) lukewarm water
2 teaspoons dry yeast
1¼ teaspoons sugar
1½ tablespoons olive oil, plus extra, for greasing
475 g (1 lb 1 oz) strong flour (see note), plus extra, for dusting
1¼ teaspoons salt

In a small bowl, mix the lukewarm water, yeast and sugar together until combined, then leave in a warm place for 5 minutes or until frothy. Stir in the olive oil.

Sift the strong flour and salt together into a large bowl. Pour the yeast mixture over the dry ingredients and use your hands to bring the mixture together to form a dough. Turn the dough out onto a work surface and use the heel of your hands to work the dough for 5 minutes until it is smooth and elastic.

Lightly grease the inside of a clean dry bowl with oil and place the dough inside. Place a tea towel (dish towel) over the dough and leave in a warm place to prove for 45–60 minutes or until doubled in size.

Dust a clean work surface lightly with the extra flour and tip out the dough. Use your fists to knock the dough back with one good punch to let any air out.

Before you portion the dough into separate balls, refer to the pizza recipe you want to make for correct measures.

Once you've separated your dough into portions, and working with one portion at a time, use the palm of your hands to cup the dough and roll it on the work surface in a circular motion to form a perfect ball. Repeat with the remaining dough portions.

Place the dough balls on a lightly greased baking tray, cover and leave in a warm place to prove for 15 minutes.

NOTE: Strong flour is very finely ground flour with a high gluten content. It is available from good delicatessens, gourmet food stores and some supermarkets. It is sometimes called '00' flour.

gluten-free pizza dough

MAKES 785 G (1 LB 11½ OZ) /
ROUGHLY ENOUGH FOR FOUR
30 CM (12 INCH) PIZZAS

450 g (1 lb oz/3 cups) gluten-free
flour, plus extra, for dusting
¼ teaspoon bicarbonate of soda
(baking soda)
1 teaspoon salt
2 teaspoons sugar
2 eggs, lightly beaten
80 ml (2½ fl oz/¼ cup) extra virgin
olive oil, plus extra, for greasing
140 ml (4¾ fl oz) lukewarm water

Lightly grease a 30 cm (12 inch) pizza tray. Sift together the gluten-free flour, bicarbonate of soda, salt and sugar into a large bowl.

In a separate bowl, mix the eggs, olive oil and water. Add to the dry ingredients and use a fork to incorporate, then use your hands to bring the mixture together to form a dough.

Before you portion the dough into separate balls, refer to the pizza recipe you want to make for correct measures (see Note, below). Lay down a clean dry tea towel (dish towel) and dust with the extra gluten-free flour.

Working with one portion of dough at a time, use your hands to gently press and flatten the dough as much as you can. Try to keep the dough as round as possible and then using a rolling pin, roll out to fit the prepared pizza tray. You will find that as this dough has no gluten, the dough will not have the elasticity of regular pizza dough and will therefore not be as easy to handle.

Lay your pizza tray upside down on the rolled-out dough and quickly flip it over, using the tea towel (dish towel) to help, so that you end up with a dough-lined pizza tray. It is now ready for the topping of your choice.

NOTE: As there is less elasticity in this dough compared to a regular dough, when a recipe calls for 170 g (6 oz), increase the dough portions by about 10 per cent to 190 g (6¾ oz). This will help prevent tearing when you need to roll out the dough to fit a standard 30 cm (12 inch) pizza tray.

pizza sauce

MAKES 420 ML (14½ FL OZ/
1⅔ CUPS)

400 g (14 oz) tin whole peeled
tomatoes
¼ teaspoon salt
1 teaspoon dried oregano
2 pinches of freshly ground black
pepper

Place all the ingredients in a food processor and blend until smooth.

NOTE: This sauce can be stored in an airtight container in the fridge for up to a week or in the freezer for up to 3 months.

veggies & sides

As you've probably noticed, I'm a big fan of vegetables and they make up a huge part of my diet. When my kids were young they had a few fussy moments with veggies. What really made the difference was getting them involved with growing, choosing and preparing vegetables for lunches and dinners. Only then did they start eating those side dishes and salads with gusto. In this chapter I'm sharing a few of the recipes that I've found to be 'sure things'. I've made the barbecued corn with chilli and lime (page 220) more times than I can count, and probably never had any leftovers and the same can be said for my cauliflower, bacon, taleggio and breadcrumb recipe (page 222). Even the most anti-cauliflower dinner guests find a way to clean their plates when this dish is on it. I hope you get the same results.

This would have to be my favourite salad to serve; it is full of flavour, looks great and makes a great complement to anything fried (especially the panko-crumbed fish on page 187). The bitter leaves and acidity of the vinegar cut through any rich or oily dishes.

radicchio salad with croutons, & balsamic vinegar

SERVES 4

Preheat the oven to 180°C (350°F/Gas 4). Cut the bread into 1 cm (¾ inch) cubes, spread over a baking tray and bake for 4–5 minutes, or until golden brown.

Whisk together the garlic, mustard, balsamic vinegar and vinegar in a small bowl. Mix in the oil and season with salt and pepper.

Separate the radicchio leaves, making sure to discard any wilted ones, and soak them in cold water for 10 minutes. Drain and dry the leaves (if you want to keep them for a while before serving, cover with a damp tea towel and refrigerate).

Roughly chop the radicchio and toss well with the croutons, vinaigrette and a third of the parmesan. Sprinkle with the rest of the cheese before serving.

a few slices of white bread (I like to use sourdough)
¼ teaspoon minced garlic
1 teaspoon dijon mustard
1 tablespoon balsamic vinegar
1 tablespoon sherry or red wine vinegar
3 tablespoons extra virgin olive oil
3 heads of radicchio, halved and cored
65 g (2¼ oz/⅔ cup) grated parmesan

I hated brussels sprouts as a child, probably more than any other food in the world. With retrospect, I don't think it was the sprouts I hated, it was how they were cooked. Now, if I'd been given them like this when I was eight years old (perhaps without the chilli) things might have been very different. I also like boiling sprouts until they're just tender, then tossing them in a brown butter sauce with some chopped parsley and lemon. These are delicious served with the twice-cooked duck with figs on page 259.

roasted brussels sprouts with chilli & speck

SERVES 4

100 g (3½ oz) cubed speck or
   pancetta, cut into largish pieces
20 brussels sprouts
2 tablespoons butter
a pinch of chilli flakes
zest of 1 lemon

Preheat the oven to 180°C (350°F/Gas 4). Put the speck in a roasting tin and cook for 10 minutes. Cut a deep cross in the bottom of each sprout so they cook evenly and take in the flavours.

Put the sprouts in the roasting tin with the speck. Add the butter, season with salt and pepper and roast for 20 minutes. Scatter with the chilli flakes and lemon zest to serve.

I remember my first trip to Indonesia about twenty years ago — it was the first time I had used my passport since my mum and dad took me on a trip around the world when I was one, so I was thrilled to explore a different culture and try their cuisine. I still recall my first taste of gado gado, mi goreng and chicken satay cooked on the side of the road and nasi goreng for breakfast. The one thing that stood out the most was the barbecued corn cooked in the little side streets by locals on their makeshift bikes with a barbecue attached. Talk about the simple things in life! Barbecued corn with chilli butter and a cold Bintang beer, watching the sun set…

corn on the barbecue with chilli & lime

SERVES 4

Place the corn cobs in cold water and soak for 10–20 minutes. Peel back (but don't remove) the husks from the cobs. Remove and discard the silk, then bring the husks back over the cob.

Preheat the barbecue to medium and grill the corn for 15–20 minutes, turning frequently, until the husks are dry and brown,

Meanwhile, combine the butter with the chilli, coriander, Tabasco and sea salt.

Peel back the husk, brush on the butter, mix liberally and cook for a further minute on the barbecue until it blackens in places, then remove from the heat and baste with more butter. Serve with lime wedges.

4 corn cobs in their husks
125 g (4½ oz) butter, softened
1 teaspoon chilli flakes
2 tablespoons chopped coriander (cilantro)
Tabasco, to taste (about 10-20 drops)
lime wedges, to serve

I don't know what it is about cauliflower with cheese but something special happens when those two ingredients get together. I definitely remember cauliflower and cheese bakes on the table when I was growing up, and this is my slightly more sophisticated version of that family favourite. Taleggio is a great cheese for this; it often has a strong aroma, but the flavour is actually quite a bit softer and it melts beautifully in this bake. The finished dish is great as a side, and so tasty you might have to hold yourself back from eating it as a main!

cauliflower with bacon, taleggio & breadcrumbs

SERVES 4

Bring a large saucepan of salted water to the boil, add the cauliflower and cook for 4 minutes or until just tender. Drain and place the cauliflower in a greased ceramic baking dish.

Meanwhile, heat a frying pan over medium heat and add the onion and pancetta. Cook for 3–4 minutes until just starting to change colour, then add the parsley. Spoon over the cauliflower.

Preheat the oven to 180°C (350°F/Gas 4). Melt the butter in a saucepan over medium heat. Stir in the flour and cook over low heat, stirring continuously. Gradually add the milk, stirring all the time, and bring to the boil. Add the taleggio and stir until melted. Season and add the nutmeg, mustard and half the parmesan, then stir until melted.

Pour the sauce over the cauliflower. Sprinkle with the remaining parmesan and the breadcrumbs. Bake for 15 minutes, or until golden.

1 cauliflower, cut into florets
1 onion, peeled and finely chopped
100 g (3½ oz) pancetta or bacon, finely chopped
2 tablespoons chopped parsley
40 g (1½ oz) butter
40 g (1½ oz) plain (all-purpose) flour
425 ml (15 fl oz/1¾ cups) milk
100 g (3½ oz) taleggio, broken into pieces
a pinch of nutmeg
1 teaspoon dijon mustard
25 g (1 oz/¼ cup) grated parmesan
25 g (1 oz/⅓ cup) fresh breadcrumbs

I love the fact that my barbecue at home has a wok burner (or an additional separate burner) on the side that allows me to either have a sauce simmering away to serve with grilled fish or meat, or, better still, create stir-fried Asian dishes outdoors. This is one of my favourite dishes to cook as a side dish to accompany anything from Southeast Asia. If you can't find water spinach, just use bok choy or choy sum instead.

wok-fried asian vegetables

SERVES 4

1 large bunch, about 1 kg (2 lb 4 oz), water spinach or any Asian green
1 tablespoon brown bean sauce or soy sauce
1 tablespoon grated palm sugar (jaggery) or soft brown sugar (optional)
3 tablespoons coconut oil
8 garlic cloves, peeled and chopped
as many long red chillies as you can tolerate, sliced
2 tablespoons fish sauce

Wash the water spinach several times. Remove the woody bottoms, then cut into 5 cm (2 inch) lengths.

Place the wok on the flame over high heat until smoking. If you are going to cook this dish indoors, you will need a commercial-quality rangehood.

Put the water spinach in a bowl, add the brown bean sauce, sugar (if using), oil, garlic and chillies and mix to combine.

When you are satisfied that your wok is red-hot, stand clear and hurl the contents of the bowl into it. You should get a spectacular explosion of flame. When it dies down, stir madly for a minute or so, gradually adding the fish sauce. Once the greens have wilted, serve immediately.

The humble cabbage is an underrated and underused vegetable, which is hard to understand as cabbages are cheap and available all year round. This crunchy, easy, healthy coleslaw is a good alternative to a leafy salad. You can use red or white cabbages or a combination of both and change the herbs to create your own version. This salad will work with just about anything off the barbecue — fish, chicken or steak. For extra crunch, toss in some crisp-fried shallots at the last minute.

asian Coleslaw

SERVES 4

DRESSING
80 ml (2½ fl oz/⅓ cup) extra virgin
  olive oil
1 tablespoon olive or coconut oil
50 ml (1½ fl oz) light soy sauce
1½ tablespoons organic honey
1 tablespoon mirin
juice of 1 lemon

½ savoy cabbage, finely shredded
¼ purple cabbage, finely shredded
4 Lebanese (short) cucumbers, halved
  lengthways, seeds removed and
  thinly sliced
2 carrots, coarsely grated
1 bunch of mint, leaves washed and
  picked
1 bunch of coriander (cilantro), leaves
  washed and picked
1 tablespoon white sesame seeds,
  toasted
1 tablespoon black sesame seeds

To make the dressing, whisk together all the ingredients and season with salt and freshly ground black pepper. Set aside.

Combine the cabbage and season with sea salt. Add the dressing, then gently toss through the cucumber, carrot, mint and coriander. To finish, sprinkle with white and black sesame seeds.

This recipe probably doesn't belong in a cookbook since we are only using three main ingredients — potatoes, garlic and rosemary — but this is something I cook at least once every fortnight with a roast. There are few things more comforting than crispy roast potatoes and beautiful roasted garlic: and you'll discover that every time you make this the potatoes disappear faster than you can say, 'pass the potatoes'!

roasted potatoes with garlic & rosemary

SERVES 4

Preheat the oven to 180°C (350°F/Gas 4). Line a large roasting tin with baking paper.

Put the potatoes in a saucepan of cold water and bring to the boil. Cook on the boil for 5 minutes, then drain.

Place the potatoes, rosemary, garlic and oil into the roasting tin and mix until the oil coats the potatoes. Season with salt and freshly ground black pepper. Cover with foil and place in the oven and cook for 30 minutes.

Remove the foil and toss the potatoes so they will cook evenly. Return to the oven without the foil and allow to cook for a further 15 minutes, or until tender in the middle and crispy on the outside. Once cooked, season with more salt and freshly ground black pepper and arrange on a large dish to serve.

900 g (2 lb) large new potatoes cut into 2.5 cm (1 inch) dice, skins on
1 bunch of rosemary, leaves picked
2 bulbs of garlic, cloves separated, skins left on
100 ml (3½ fl oz) coconut or olive oil

I'm always looking for ways to make the dinner table a healthier and more interesting place, not only for myself but for my kids. A good way of achieving this is through the use of salads — this is a wonderful salad that includes some of the world's wonder foods: quinoa, red rice and nuts. Red rice is a wholegrain rice renowned for its delicious flavour and excellent health benefits. Its red colouring is the result of natural pigments contained in its pericap. This salad is a tasty accompaniment to meals from nearly every cuisine. Don't stick to my recipe — have some fun with the ingredients and create your own super salad!

quinoa, red rice, carrot & pistachio salad

SERVES 4

100g (3½ oz) Camargue red rice
  (see note)
100 g (3½ oz/½ cup) quinoa
2 tablespoons coconut or olive oil
1 brown onion, peeled and finely
  sliced
60 g (2¼ oz) pistachios
1 large carrot, grated
100 g (3½ oz/2 cups) baby English
  spinach leaves, thinly sliced
4 spring onions (scallions), thinly
  sliced
100 g (3½ oz) dried apricots, roughly
  chopped
1 handful of mint

DRESSING
90 ml (3 fl oz) extra virgin olive oil
finely grated zest and juice of 1
  orange
2 teaspoons lemon juice
1 garlic clove, peeled and minced

Preheat the oven to 180°C (350°F/Gas 4).

Cook the red rice in boiling salted water for 45 minutes, or until cooked. Drain and allow to cool. At the same time, bring a large saucepan of water to the boil, add the quinoa and simmer for 12–14 minutes, or until cooked. Drain and allow to cool.

Meanwhile, heat the oil in a small saucepan over medium heat and cook the onion, stirring occasionally, for 10–15 minutes, or until soft and caramelised. At the same time, place the pistachios on a baking tray and cook in the oven for 8 minutes, or until lightly toasted. Roughly chop.

To make the dressing, combine the ingredients and set aside.

Place the quinoa, rice and onion in a large bowl, add the remaining ingredients, drizzle with the dressing and mix together to completely coat with the dressing.

NOTE: Camargue red rice is available from speciality food stores. You can use brown rice or wild rice instead of Camargue.

showing off

I was going to call this chapter 'entertaining', but then I thought, 'Nah! Let's be honest and call it what it is: showing off!' I won't lie; some of these dishes (like the tea-smoked duck breast with foie gras ravioli) do take a bit of time and concentration. But if you're determined to impress and up for a challenge these recipes will really deliver. They'll also get easier the more you make them, and may even become a regular feature at your dinner parties. If you're going for rustic and hearty, the paella on page 252 is colourful, festive and perfect for a crowd. You could even go all out on the Spanish theme by starting the night off with a few tapas, and uncorking some Spanish sherry. If elegance and sophistication is what you're after, a starter of tartare (page 240) followed by the barbecued marron (page 267) will really blow people away.

Teague Ezard's eponymous restaurant in Melbourne has always been a standout for me — he is a chef who has a great take on flavours as well as presentation. It was while filming with him a few years ago that he taught me this amazing concoction. I was truly blown away, not just because of the wasabi in the mix (you can play with that to see how much kick you want), but also because of how elegant and simple the recipe actually was. This is why I have to feature it in this book — it really is a killer way to serve oysters!

japanese-inspired oyster shooter with sake, mirin & wasabi

SERVES 4

Place the mirin and sake in a small saucepan over a high heat and burn off the alcohol. When ready, remove from the heat and set aside to cool. Once cool, strain, add the rice vinegar and taste for a balance of sweet and sour. Add the light soy sauce for colour and flavour, then add the wasabi powder, mixing well to combine. Refrigerate until the wasabi powder has fallen to the bottom and you are left with a clear liquid.

Strain the liquid into a jug making sure not to disturb the impurities at the bottom and refrigerate until needed.

Serve in shot glasses, first placing an oyster in each glass and then pouring over some of the shooter mix.

SHOOTER MIX
500 ml (17 fl oz/2 cups) mirin
125 ml (4 fl oz/½ cup) sake
35 ml (1 fl oz) rice vinegar
1 tablespoon light soy sauce
1 tablespoon wasabi powder

20 freshly shucked oysters

For me, the best type of meat besides pork, duck, chicken, beef, kangaroo, quail, rabbit and venison would have to be lamb … okay, okay, I love them all. You can't make a chef choose a favourite meat. That said, I do love lamb in all its forms; from the tender rack, tasty rump, the mouthwatering roast leg of lamb to deep-fried brains. This is one of the best ways I have prepared it over the past few years. Minced lamb is a great option for your next barbie because it's easy to make it look really impressive but you won't have to take out a second mortgage to get all the ingredients.

spiced lamb skewers with pomegranate molasses

SERVES 4

400 g (14 oz) low-fat minced (ground) lamb
1 garlic clove, peeled and minced
1 tomato, seeded and finely diced
1 teaspoon pomegranate molasses, plus extra, to serve
seeds of 1 pomegranate, to serve
mint leaves, to serve

TURKISH SPICE MIX
35 g (1¼ oz/⅓ cup) ground cumin
3 tablespoons (¼ oz) dried mint
3 tablespoons (¼ oz) dried oregano
2 tablespoons sweet paprika
2 tablespoons cracked black pepper
2 teaspoons hot paprika

POMEGRANATE YOGHURT
125 g (4½ oz/½ cup) plain yoghurt
2 tablespoons pomegranate molasses
1 small handful of mint, chopped
1 teaspoon sumac

Soak 8 bamboo skewers in water overnight or use metal skewers.

To make the Turkish spice mix, combine all the ingredients and store in an airtight container until needed.

Combine the lamb with the garlic, tomato, pomegranate molasses and 1 tablespoon of the Turkish spice then mix thoroughly and season with sea salt and cracked black pepper. Shape the lamb around the skewers and refrigerate for 30 minutes to set before cooking.

Combine the yoghurt with the pomegranate molasses, mint and sumac.

Preheat a barbecue hotplate or grill pan to medium. Add the skewers and cook for 3 minutes, then turn and cook for a further 3 minutes or until cooked through.

Serve with the yoghurt sauce, pomegranate seeds and mint. If you like, you can drizzle a bit more pomegranate molasses over the lamb once it is cooked.

NOTE: You can keep any remaining Turkish spice mix in an airtight container for up to a month.

This has become somewhat of a signature dish for me whenever I entertain. All I know is that whether I serve it as a finger-food or a first course, it knocks everyone's socks off every time. It is great on its own, or with a touch of chilli oil and a bit of finely sliced basil. My favourite way to serve it is to put amazing seafood in a bowl or cup, pour over the hot soup and finish with some baby herbs. The best seafood for this, in no particular order, is shaved abalone, seared scallops, steamed mussels, vongole or clams, hand-picked crabmeat, pan-roasted bug tails, fried soft shell crab or smoked trout.

sweet corn soup with mussels, basil & chilli

SERVES 4 AS A MAIN, 20
AS A STARTER

Remove the kernels from the corn cobs (you should have about 1.5 kg (3 lb 5 oz) of kernels) and set aside for the soup.

Use the peeled corn cobs to make a corn stock, place them in a large pot with the onion, garlic and 4 litres (140 fl oz) of water. Bring to the boil, simmer for an hour and then remove from the heat. Allow the stock to cool for a further hour and then strain, discarding the corn cobs and reserving the corn stock to use in the soup.

To open the mussels, place them in a heated pot with a splash of water and cover with a tight-fitting lid. Cook for 2 minutes or until the mussels have opened. Remove from the heat and discard any mussels that remain closed.

Remove the mussel meat from the shells and reserve and strain any cooking liquor for the soup.

Heat the butter in a saucepan and gently cook the shallots and garlic until soft and translucent. Add the corn kernels and cook for another couple of minutes then add the wine, corn stock and cooking liquid from the mussels. Bring to the boil, reduce the heat and simmer for 20 minutes. Add the cream and cook for another 2 minutes then remove from the heat and blend until smooth. Pass through a sieve and season with salt.

Place the mussels into the bottom of small serving cups. Pour the soup over the mussels and top with the chilli oil and basil.

10 corn cobs
1 onion, halved
3 garlic cloves
20 mussels, cleaned, beards removed
50 g (1¾ oz) butter
6 large French shallots, peeled and sliced
4 cloves garlic, peeled and sliced
100 ml (3½ fl oz) white wine
100 ml (3½ fl oz) pouring cream
2 teaspoons chilli oil, to serve
½ punnet baby purple basil, trimmed or 4 basil leaves, finely shredded, to serve

When I got my first job in television I was talking to the head honchos about the type of show they wanted to make. I was a bit nervous about what they were going to ask of me in a culinary way — I was still defining my own style within my restaurants. I needn't have worried because they let me have free reign for five years. However, there was one stipulation: 'Pete, you can do whatever you want, just no bloody seared tuna salads'. I promised I wouldn't do one on the show, and I stayed true to my word. Many years later, while writing a book, I decided it was time to include one and this is still one of my favourites today.

seared tuna with wakame & ponzu salad

SERVES 4

1 tablespoon sichuan peppercorns
1 tablespoon black peppercorns
1 tablespoon sea salt
8 tablespoons fresh wakame
   seaweed
1 telegraph cucumber, cut into
   ribbons using a vegetable peeler,
   juice saved for dressing
90 g (3¼ oz/1 cup) daikon, julienned
1 long red chilli, julienned
1 tablespoon flying fish roe
4 x 120 g (4¼ oz) pieces tuna, either
   yellowfin or bluefin

TANGY PONZU DRESSING
2 free-range egg yolks
1 free-range egg
100 ml (3½ fl oz) ponzu (see note)
400 ml (14 fl oz) olive oil
100 ml (3½ fl oz) reserved
   cucumber juice
juice of 1 lime

Preheat a barbecue hotplate or grill to high, dry-roast the sichuan and black peppercorns and salt in a small frying pan on the hotplate for a few minutes or until fragrant. Grind in a mortar and pestle until fine.

To make the dressing, blend the yolks, whole egg and ponzu with a hand blender. With the motor still running, slowly add the oil to form a mayonnaise. Add the reserved cucumber juice and lime juice and season with salt and pepper.

Mix the seaweed, cucumber, daikon and chilli together with some of the dressing.

Roll the tuna pieces in the spices and sear on the preheated hotplate for 2 minutes on each side. Cut the tuna into pieces and top with the salad and fish roe. Serve the remaining dressing on the side.

NOTE: Ponzu is a Japanese soy, citrus and vinegar dressing and is available from Japanese supermarkets.

Jacinta Cannataci is a great friend and one-half of the Cannataci twins. Monica and Jacinta worked with me for nearly a decade, and I am the luckiest chef in the world to have worked with them. This tuna tartare recipe is one of Jacinta's. It's a great one because it is simple to make but looks like a lot of work has gone into creating it.

tuna tartare on potato crisp

MAKES 20

To make the potato crisps, thinly slice the potatoes on a mandolin, wash in cold water to remove some of the starch and pat dry with kitchen paper. Heat the oil to 160°C (315°F) in a wok or deep saucepan, fry the potato slices on both sides until light golden, drain on kitchen paper and sprinkle with sea salt.

To make the tomato chutney, heat the olive oil in a saucepan over medium heat, add the mustard seeds and onion and cook until lightly brown. Add the garlic, chilli, ginger and turmeric and cook until fragrant. Add the tomato and cook until softened then add the red wine vinegar and sugar if using. Cook until the liquid has reduced by half. Season with salt and pepper and cool.

Dice the tuna into small pieces and place in a chilled bowl. Finely chop 3 of the green beans, add to the tuna with 3 tablespoons of the tomato chutney, the olives and basil and mix until combined. Season with salt and pepper.

Spoon a teaspoon of the tuna mix on a potato crisp, finely slice the remaining green beans on an angle and sprinkle over the top.

200 g (7 oz) best-quality sashimi tuna, (or salmon or kingfish)
5 green beans, blanched
50 g (1¾ oz) dried Kalamata olives, pitted and diced
4 basil leaves, finely shredded

POTATO CRISPS
4 kipfler potatoes, peeled
olive oil for deep-frying

TOMATO CHUTNEY
1 tablespoon extra virgin olive oil
1 tablespoon yellow mustard seeds
1 onion, peeled and chopped
3 garlic cloves, peeled and chopped
1 long red chilli, chopped
1 tablespoon ground ginger
1 tablespoon ground turmeric
6 vine-ripened tomatoes, diced
50 ml (1½ fl oz) red wine vinegar
50 g (1¾ oz) caster (superfine) sugar (optional)

I'd just completed my culinary duties for G'Day USA — an American/Australian art and culture promotion in New York — when I met up with Monica Duggan at the Consulate-General of Australia's farewell do. After a glass or two of fine champagne, Monica let me in on her family's secret recipe for making borscht. Since then she has cooked it for me and it is wonderful. It rightly deserves a place in this book. Thanks, Monica, I owe you one!

monica's beetroot borscht with crème fraîche & dill

SERVES 4 AS A MAIN,
20 AS A STARTER

1 kg (2 lb 4 oz) beef bone marrow
1 dried bay leaf
½ small white cabbage, shredded
1 small potato, diced
1 carrot, finely diced
20 g (¾ oz) butter
½ onion, peeled and finely chopped
2 garlic cloves, peeled and chopped
1 bunch large beetroot, peeled and
    finely shredded
2½ tablespoons red wine vinegar
½ teaspoon caster (superfine) sugar
    (optional)
125 g (4½ oz) tinned chopped
    tomatoes
½ small celeriac, finely diced
½ parsnip, finely diced
½ turnip, finely diced
80 g (2¾ oz/⅓ cup) crème fraîche,
    to serve
dill sprigs, to serve

Place the bone marrow in a large saucepan with 1 litre (35 fl oz/4 cups) water, bay leaf and some salt to make a stock. Simmer for 30 minutes, skimming occasionally, and then strain.

Return the stock to medium heat, add the cabbage, bring to the boil, then add the potato and carrot then simmer partly covered for 30 minutes.

Meanwhile, in a separate saucepan, melt the butter over low heat, add the onion and garlic and cook until just translucent. Add the beetroot, red wine vinegar, sugar (if using), tomatoes and a little salt and pepper. Add the celeriac, parsnip and turnip. Pour in the marrow stock and cabbage and gently simmer until all the vegetables are tender. Do not boil as the soup will lose its colour. Serve in small bowls topped with a spoonful of crème fraîche and dill sprigs.

I was invited to cater for the Prince and Princess of Denmark a year or so ago and was quietly scared at the prospect — seven courses, two hundred people, and cooking in someone's mansion. John Pye, my head chef at the time, was tinkering with a variation on prawn cocktail using lobster and mango. When he had finally perfected the dish, I thought we should serve it to the royals — well a girl from Tassie should love a bit of local rock lobster, don't you think? If lobster is a bit hard to come by, prawns, crabmeat or bugs would also be beautiful.

lobster martini

Have 4 martini glasses ready.

Mix together all the coconut dressing ingredients.

Mix the mango, coconut flesh, chilli, lime juice and Thai basil together to make the salsa. Spoon 2 tablespoons of salsa into the bottom of each martini glass.

Slice the lobster into 1 cm (½ inch) thick medallions (you should have about 12 of them). Put three slices of lobster in each glass, then dress with the coconut dressing. Add a touch more salsa on top and finish with the kaffir lime strips, red chilli and betel leaves.

SERVES 4 AS A STARTER

COCONUT DRESSING (MAKES ABOUT 185 ML (6 FL OZ/¾ CUP)
150 ml (5 fl oz) coconut cream
2 tablespoons lime juice
1 tablespoon fish sauce

MANGO SALSA
1–2 ripe mangoes, peeled and diced
6 tablespoons finely diced young coconut flesh
1 long red chilli, deseeded and finely diced
juice of 2 limes
9 Thai basil leaves, julienned

1 x 1 kg (2 lb 4 oz) rock lobster, cooked and shell removed
125 ml (4 fl oz/½ cup) coconut dressing (see above)
2 kaffir lime leaves, julienned
julienned red chilli and betel leaves, to serve

I have had the good fortune in my life to meet some of my idols face to face, and the highlight so far was when Tetsuya Wakuda agreed to be a part of my fishing show. We had a wonderful day fishing off Udo's Chinese junk for flathead and snapper and then headed off to Tetsuya's restaurant with our catch. He prepared the most amazing dish I have ever tried in my life and I'm very honoured that he agreed to share it with me all those years ago. Thanks, Tets.

tetsuya's warm flathead carpaccio with black bean dressing

SERVES 4 AS A STARTER

4 tablespoons dried wakame
  seaweed
200 g (7 oz) flathead fillet, skin off
  and pinboned (you could also use
  kingfish, jewfish or snapper)
lots of ground white pepper
4 tablespoons finely julienned fresh
  ginger
4 tablespoons olive oil
1 bunch of coriander, with roots
  and stalks
2½ tablespoons soy sauce
3 tablespoons mirin
100 ml (3½ fl oz) chicken stock
2 teaspoons chopped salted
  fermented black beans
½ garlic clove, minced
1 teaspoon chopped chilli
1 small bacon rasher, finely julienned
2 spring onions, white part only,
  finely sliced
grated zest of 1 orange
4 spring onions, green part only,
  finely sliced
2 tablespoons snipped chives

Preheat the oven to 150°C (300°F/Gas 2). Soak the wakame seaweed in water for 10 minutes to soften it, then drain.

Make sure you remove any skin from the flathead. Starting at the tail, slice the flathead paper-thin on an angle. Lay the fish out, slightly overlapping, on a platter or individual plates. Season with lots of freshly ground white pepper and the ginger. Drizzle with the olive oil to coat the fish lightly.

Put the plate in the oven for 2–3 minutes, or until the plate is hot and the fish is just starting to cook slightly (but still rare to raw).

Prepare the coriander: finely chop the roots and measure out 1 teaspoonful. Finely chop the stalks and measure out 1 teaspoonful. Keep the leaves whole — you will need a small handful.

To make the dressing, heat the soy, mirin and chicken stock until simmering. Add the black beans, garlic, chilli and coriander root. Cut the bacon into julienne strips (you need about 2 tablespoons) and add to the pan. Remove from the heat and add the coriander stalks.

Drizzle some warm dressing over the fish and then top with the seaweed, white spring onion and orange zest. Spoon some more dressing over these and then finish with the green spring onions, coriander leaves and chives.

This may be the most popular finger food in the world — created by the Chinese in the 1300s and perfected over the next 700 odd years — I'd say you're in trusted hands with this dish. It is always a crowd-pleaser and the best part is it's so easy to make. You can buy everything you need in Chinatown or your local Asian grocer.

peking duck rolls — my way

MAKES 20

To make the pancakes, combine the flours in a bowl, make a well in the centre and whisk in the milk, eggs, half the butter and 80 ml (2½ fl oz/⅓ cup) water. Whisk until the batter is smooth. Pour into a jug. Cover and stand for 15 minutes.

Heat a small non-stick frying pan over low–medium heat. Brush with the remaining butter. Pour 2 tablespoons of batter into the frying pan and spread to form a thin pancake about 15 cm (6 inches) in diameter. Cook for 2 minutes. Turn and cook for a further minute. Transfer to a plate. Repeat with the remaining batter adding a little more milk if it gets too thick. Cool the pancakes and shred 2 of them to use as garnish. Use the remaining pancakes cut in half to serve with the duck.

Remove the skin and meat from the cooked duck. Thinly slice both the skin and meat. Combine the hoisin and plum sauces. Lay 20 lettuce leaves on platters and top with some shredded duck meat and skin, spring onion and cucumber. To serve, spoon over some of the sauce, sprinkle with the sesame seeds and top with the shredded pancake.

PANCAKE
75 g (2½ oz/½ cup) plain
   (all-purpose) flour
2 tablespoons cornflour (cornstarch)
60 ml (2 fl oz/¼ cup) milk
2 free-range eggs
40 g (1½ oz) butter, melted

1 Peking duck (from a Chinese
   barbecue shop)
200 ml (7 fl oz) hoisin sauce
50 ml (1½ fl oz) plum sauce
4 baby cos (romaine) lettuces,
   leaves separated and washed
6 spring onions (scallions), cut
   into batons
2 cucumbers, cut into batons
1½ tablespoons toasted sesame
   seeds

This dish really defines my preferred cooking style — super-easy but full of flavour. Originally, the Italians cooked the fish in seawater, which is where the name crazy water or 'aqua pazza' comes from. Today we use sparkling mineral water and salt.

snapper aqua pazza (fish in crazy water)

SERVES 4

4 frying-pan or plate-sized snappers, bream, mullet, garfish or whiting, scaled and gutted
12 cloves garlic confit, page 108
4 tablespoons chilli confit, page 191
20 cherry tomatoes
20 Ligurian olives (or marinated small olives), pitted
1.5 litres (52 fl oz/6 cups) sparkling mineral water
3 tablespoons butter
24 basil leaves

Make three cuts down to the bone on both sides of each fish and then cook each fish separately, using a quarter of the ingredients for each one. (You might want to keep the cooked fish in a warm oven as you go.)

Heat a touch of olive oil in a frying pan, add the fish and cook for 3–4 minutes until golden on one side. Turn the fish over and add the confit of garlic and chilli, the tomatoes and olives and season with sea salt and cracked pepper. After 30 seconds add the mineral water (just enough to cover the fish), butter and basil and cook for another couple of minutes until the fish is just cooked through.

Lift out onto a serving plate and pour the sauce over the top.

On my travels around Spain I was blown away by the many versions of paella I tasted. It's one of the country's iconic dishes, and though there is a fairly standard base recipe, each town, village and cook seems to have their own variation. This is mine. In the simplest terms, paella is one big happy surf and turf rice dish. The shallow two-handled pan or 'paella' gives the dish its name, and although you could easily make yours in a large wide saucepan, an authentic paella pan isn't very expensive and looks great on the middle of the table.

paella

SERVES 4

Preheat your oven to 180°C (350°F/Gas 4). Put the stock in a saucepan over heat and add the parsley stalks, the prawn shells and heads and half the lemon. Bring to a simmer and add the saffron.

Heat a touch of oil in a frying pan and fry the garlic, tomatoes and paprika for a few minutes until soft, then purée with a blender or pound in a mortar and pestle. (This mixture is called picada.)

Heat the oil in a paella pan or large heavy-based frying pan and fry the chorizo on both sides. Add the rice and the picada and cook for a few minutes, stirring well.

Strain the hot stock into the paella pan and stir well. Add a touch of sea salt, bring to the boil for 5 minutes and then stir again.

Add the squid, vongole and prawns to the paella pan, cover with the lid or foil and put in the oven for 15 minutes, or until the rice is cooked and the clams have opened. Arrange the pimento or capsicum strips over the top with the chopped parsley and lemon zest. Season with sea salt and cracked pepper if needed and serve immediately in the paella pan.

750 ml (26 fl oz/3 cups) fish or chicken stock
10 flat-leaf (Italian) parsley stalks
250 g (9 oz) peeled prawns (shells and heads kept)
1 lemon, zested and then cut in half
a pinch of saffron threads
2½ tablespoons extra virgin olive oil
2 garlic cloves, peeled and minced
2 ripe tomatoes, chopped
1 teaspoon smoked paprika (I like to use La Chinata)
1 chorizo sausage, cut into 1 cm (½ inch) slices
250 g (9 oz) Calasparra or Bomba short-grain rice
150 g (5½ oz) cleaned and scored squid, cut into bite-sized pieces
100 g (3½ oz) surf clams, mussels or pipis
75 g (2¾ oz) pimentos or roasted capsicum, cut into strips
a handful of chopped flat-leaf (Italian) parsley

Hot and sour is a Chinese term for dishes flavoured with chilli, white pepper, sesame oil, garlic, ginger and vinegar. This soup is so nourishing and full of flavour on a cold night that you'll want seconds, and thirds. The white pepper creates a beautiful and unique flavour. If you have a Chinatown where you live, you should be able to pick up some beautiful cooked pork, which makes this soup really straightforward and easy.

hot and sour soup with crabmeat & tofu

SERVES 4

75 g (2¾ oz) cooked pork loin
   or Chinese roast pork
200 g (7 oz) picked crabmeat
   (spanner, blue swimmer, mud
   or king crab)
2 tablespoons finely sliced bamboo
   shoots
1 tablespoon cornflour
1 litre (35 fl oz/4 cups) chicken stock
8 shiitake mushrooms, stalks
   removed, finely sliced
4 wood-ear mushrooms, julienned
100 g (3½ oz) silken tofu, diced
1 tablespoon Shaoxing rice wine
2 tablespoons light soy sauce
2 tablespoons Chinese black vinegar
25 g (1 oz) vermicelli rice noodles
2 free-range eggs, lightly beaten
2 teaspoons white pepper
2 tablespoons finely chopped spring
   onion
chopped coriander leaves
1 teaspoon each of sesame oil and
   chilli oil

Shred the pork finely and mix with the crab, bamboo shoots and 1 teaspoon of the cornflour in a bowl.

Bring the stock to the boil in a large saucepan. Stir in the pork mixture, then both types of mushrooms, the tofu, rice wine, soy sauce, vinegar and some sea salt. Meanwhile, soak the noodles in hot water for 5 minutes, then drain, rinse in cold water and spoon into four bowls.

Mix the rest of the cornflour with enough cold water to make a paste, add to the soup and simmer until thickened.
In a steady stream, add the beaten egg to the pan and whisk with a fork to break it up. Cook for 1 minute.

Sprinkle the white pepper into the noodle bowls, pour the soup over the top and garnish with spring onions, chopped coriander, sesame oil and chilli oil.

If I had one last dish to eat on earth, this would be it (well, it would be the starter anyway). You could also use any fresh seafood that can be eaten raw. Sea urchin, cuttlefish, scampi, scallop or prawn would be as delicious. It is a mixture of Japanese and Korean flavours and words cannot really do it justice.

bibimbap sushi

SERVES 4

To make the sushi rice, put the sugar, salt and vinegar in a pan and heat gently until dissolved. Cook the rice with 330 ml (11 fl oz/1⅓ cups) of water, following the instructions on the packet, in a saucepan, rice cooker or microwave. Spread the hot cooked rice in a large tray and pour the rice vinegar dressing over it. Stir with chopsticks or a fork to cool the rice down and distribute the dressing evenly. Place a damp cloth over the rice until you're ready to use it. This should be eaten the day it is made, and not refrigerated — I like it best when it's just above room temperature.

Blanch the bean sprouts in boiling salted water for 30 seconds and then refresh under cold water. Mix together the rice wine vinegar, soy, salt, sugar (if using) and chilli powder and pour over the bean sprouts to make pickled bean sprouts. Leave to marinate for 20 minutes and then drain.

Place the rice in the bottom of four bowls or martini glasses. Make a small indentation in the rice and place the quail yolk into this. Top with half the sesame seeds and then dot the mayonnaise over the rice. Top with the bean sprouts, then the cucumber, then the fish. Drizzle the tamari soy sauce and wasabi over the fish, sprinkle with the rest of the sesame seeds, then top with the caviar and finally the nori. Serve with pickled ginger.

SUSHI RICE

2 tablespoons caster (superfine) sugar (optional)
1 teaspoon sea salt
2 tablespoons rice vinegar (or ponzu-flavoured vinegar)
225 g (8 oz/1 cup) short-grain rice, washed thoroughly

a handful of bean sprouts
3 tablespoons rice wine vinegar
1 tablespoon soy sauce
1 teaspoon salt
1 tablespoon caster (superfine) sugar
a pinch of chilli powder
1 quantity sushi rice (see above)
4 quail eggs, separated (you won't be using the whites)
2 teaspoons toasted sesame seeds
2 tablespoons Japanese mayonnaise (from Asian supermarkets)
a handful of julienned cucumber
160 g (5¾ oz) Spanish mackerel or kingfish, skin off, pinboned and thinly sliced
160 g (5¾ oz) bluefin, yellowfin or longtail tuna, skin off, pinboned and thinly sliced
160 g (5¾ oz) trevally, ocean trout or Atlantic salmon, skin off, pinboned and thinly sliced
tamari soy sauce
wasabi
4 tablespoons salmon caviar
1 sheet toasted nori, julienned

Duck, duck, duck! Is there a better tasting bird out there? I doubt it very much. I could devote a whole chapter to my favourite game bird but I've just included this recipe that I cook at home — it doesn't have many ingredients but it's simply delicious. The brussels sprout recipe on page 219 goes brilliantly with this. If figs are not in season use dried ones, or experiment with other fruit such as quince, orange, pear...

twice-cooked duck with figs

SERVES 4

2 x 1.8 kg (4 lb) ducks
300 g (10½ oz) soft brown sugar (optional)
500 ml (17 fl oz/2 cups) veal stock
6 fresh figs, cut into quarters
1 small handful of basil leaves
2½ tablespoons apple balsamic vinegar
2 tablespoons olive oil
200 g (7 oz) cavolo nero (or spinach or silverbeet)
juice of ½ lemon

Preheat the oven to 120°C (235°F/Gas ½). Rub the ducks with brown sugar (if using), then slow-roast in the oven for 2½ hours. Let the ducks cool slightly, then cut them down to four breasts and four legs.

Meanwhile, put the veal stock in a pan and cook over medium heat until reduced by half.

Increase the oven to 160°C (315°F/Gas 2–3). Place the duck and stock in a roasting tin and cook for a further 10–15 minutes. Add the figs, basil and apple balsamic and season with salt and pepper, then cook for a further 5 minutes.

Heat the olive oil in a frying pan over medium heat and sauté the cavolo nero until wilted. Season with sea salt and cracked pepper and add the lemon juice. Serve with the duck and figs.

This is a recipe inspired by arguably Australia's finest culinary ambassador, Neil Perry. I can remember my first visit to Rockpool about twenty years ago and this was the canapé that was served to me. Wow, what a taste sensation! This was how I wanted my food to look and taste. The next day I bought Neil's cookbook and studied each and every recipe. I have taken the liberty of simplifying the pasta recipe by using gow gee wrappers (which you can pick up in the frozen section of your supermarket or Asian grocer).

goat's curd tortellini with brown butter & muscatel raisins

MAKES 20

Combine the goat's curd, chives, lemon zest, salt and white pepper for the goat's curd filling. Place 1 teaspoon of filling in the centre of each gow gee wrapper and brush a little water around the edges. Fold over into a half-moon shape and join two corners together to form a tortellini, press to seal.

Heat the butter in a frying pan for 2–3 minutes or until it turns nut brown. Add the balsamic vinegar and then the pine nuts, sage, muscatels and some salt and pepper.

Cook the tortellini in boiling salted water for about 2 minutes or until cooked through, then lift out with a slotted spoon. Add the tortellini to the butter mixture, toss gently and sprinkle with the parmesan and serve.

200 g (7 oz) goat's curd
1 bunch chives, finely snipped
zest of 2 lemons
20 gow gee wrappers
100 g (3½ oz) butter
25 ml (1¼ fl oz) balsamic vinegar
1 tablespoon pine nuts
2 teaspoons chopped sage leaves
30 g (1 oz/¼ cup) muscatel raisins
3 tablespoons finely grated
   parmesan

Peter Kuruvita has a wonderful relationship with seafood. I filmed with Pete a couple of times over the past few years and was lucky enough to be with him the day he made his version of chilli mud crab — this is loosely based on his recipe but I have made it with lobster as I think lobster needs all the help it can get to make it taste as good as a crab (sorry, I am a crab bloke from way back). But I'm really happy with this, I think it gives lobster a moment to shine and it couldn't be faster to cook.

wok-fried lobster with mirin & chilli sauce

SERVES 4

2 live lobsters
2 long red chillies, seeded, chopped
8 cm (3¼ inch) piece of ginger, peeled and chopped
½ bunch of coriander (cilantro) including roots, chopped
200 ml (7 fl oz) light soy sauce
200 ml (7 fl oz) mirin
100 ml (3½ fl oz) white wine
1 tablespoon coconut oil
150 ml (5 fl oz) sweet chilli sauce (optional)
2 garlic cloves, peeled and chopped
½ bunch spring onions (scallions), cut into batons
1 large handful of mixed Asian herbs, such as mint, coriander (cilantro), Thai basil, Vietnamese mint
steamed jasmine rice, to serve
wok-fried Asian vegetables, to serve

Place the lobsters in the freezer for about 3–4 hours until they are dead (but not frozen through) then remove the heads, and cut in half and remove the coral (mustard looking part in the head). Cut the tails into 2.5cm (1 inch) medallions with a cleaver or heavy kitchen knife.

Blend the chillies, ginger, coriander, light soy, mirin, white wine, coconut oil, sweet chilli sauce (if using) and garlic in a food processor until finely blended.

Heat a wok to medium–high. Cook the lobster with the blended mix. Cover and cook for 5 minutes, or until the lobster turns orange and the flesh is just cooked through. Top with the spring onion and fresh herbs and serve with jasmine rice and some beautiful wok-fried Asian vegetables.

As you may be aware by now, I have two great culinary loves: Japanese food and barbecues, and I see no reason why the two should not live harmoniously in this book. This recipe is based on a dish I have eaten at many Japanese restaurants over the years and it is one I never tire of. Tataki of beef is a very briefly seared piece of meat that is then sliced and dressed with a lovely sauce. This recipe calls for the inclusion of crispy garlic chips, which really make the dish. They give it that little pop of texture and crispiness that just works with the beautiful rare beef.

japanese beef tataki

SERVES 4

Preheat the barbecue hotplate or grill to hot. Lightly brush the beef fillet with some olive oil and season with salt and pepper. Prepare an ice bath. Sear the beef on a hot barbecue hotplate or grill or in a cast-iron pan. Once coloured well on all surfaces, plunge into the ice bath and allow to cool for about 3–4 minutes. Remove and drain well. Slice the beef tataki into thin slices and arrange on the plate.

To make the onion ponzu, combine all the ingredients in a bowl.

To make the tataki dressing, combine all the ingredients in a bowl.

Slice the spring onion as finely as possible into little circles and wash under running water for a few minutes, then drain and refrigerate.

To make the crispy garlic chips. Thinly slice the garlic then heat 2 cm (¾ inch) of oil in a small deep saucepan over medium–high heat. Add the garlic and fry until golden and crispy. Remove with a slotted spoon. Drain on paper towel.

Drizzle the onion ponzu on top of the beef, then drizzle on some tataki dressing and top with the spring onion, chives and garlic.

300 g (10½ oz) beef fillet, trimmed of fat
olive oil, for cooking
2 spring onions (scallions)

CRISPY GARLIC CHIPS
4 garlic cloves, peeled
1 tablespoon finely chopped chives

ONION PONZU
1 white onion, very finely diced (as small as possible)
¼ teaspoon very finely chopped garlic (as small as possible)
3 tablespoons olive oil
1 tablespoon lemon juice
1 tablespoon rice vinegar
1 tablespoon dark soy sauce
¼ teaspoon finely chopped ginger

TATAKI DRESSING
5 tablespoons soy sauce
8 tablespoons rice vinegar
pinch of bonito flakes (optional)

The sauce in this dish is simply to die for. It works with all types of seafood but my favourite is the delicate flesh of the freshwater marron. Think of them as a large yabbie or small lobster. I'm an olive oil man myself, but the butter in this makes it spectacular.

barbecued marron with thyme, sambuca & orange butter

SERVES 4

4 West Australian marron
1 lemon, cut into wedges or cheeks

FLAVOURED BUTTER
500 ml (17 fl oz/2 cups) orange juice
250 g (9 oz) unsalted butter, chopped
finely grated zest of 1 orange
juice of 2 lemons
½ bunch of lemon thyme, chopped
1 bunch of chervil, chopped
1 teaspoon ground fennel
45 ml (1½ fl oz) white sambuca

To make the flavoured butter, place the orange juice in a saucepan over medium–high heat. Bring to the boil and simmer until reduced to about 2½ tablespoons. Set aside to cool completely. Then add the butter, zest, lemon juice, thyme, chervil, fennel and sambuca and gently melt over low heat – stirring to combine. Process until combined, then season. Roll the butter in plastic wrap to form a sausage shape and refrigerate until set.

Put the marron in the freezer for about 1 hour, or until they are unconscious.

Split the marron down the centre with a sharp, heavy knife and remove the entrails.

Preheat the barbecue hotplate to high. Cook the marron on the barbecue, flesh side down, for a couple of minutes until the flesh of the marron is just opaque and cooked through. Take them off the grill, move to a serving platter and put a few knobs of flavoured butter on top to melt. Grill the lemon and serve with the marron.

NOTE: You can freeze any remaining butter for up to a month.

Compound butters are a great accompaniment to any good barbecue. A compound butter is, very simply, butter that has been flavoured with herbs and/or spices and other condiments such as mustard, anchovies, capers etc. The butter here has loads of beautiful ingredients flecked through it and when melted over steak, it gives the most wonderful flavour and aroma. There is a café in Geneva called Café de Paris and it is renowned for its steak with Café de Paris sauce. The sauce is a trade secret but it's said to contain thyme, chicken livers, dijon mustard and cream. So this butter is a variation on that theme and is one of my favourite ways to serve steak.

sirloin steak with café de paris butter

SERVES 4

To make the Café de Paris butter, blend the tomato sauce, mustard, capers, shallots, herbs, garlic, anchovies, Cognac or brandy, Madeira, Worcestershire sauce, spices, lemon juice and citrus zests together. Cream the butter with a whisk until pale and fluffy. Mix through the blended ingredients and roll the mixture in plastic wrap to form a sausage shape. Store in the fridge or freezer until needed.

Rub the steaks with oil and season with salt and pepper and bring to room temperature. Preheat a barbecue hotplate or grill pan to high. Add the steaks and cook for a few minutes on each side until cooked to your liking. Set aside to rest topped with slices of butter. Serve with French fries and a simple salad.

NOTE: You can freeze the remaining Café de Paris butter for up to a month.

4 x 250 g (9 oz) sirloin steaks

CAFÉ DE PARIS BUTTER
1 tablespoon tomato sauce (ketchup)
1 teaspoon dijon mustard
1 teaspoon baby capers, rinsed
2 tablespoons chopped French
    shallots
2 teaspoons finely chopped parsley
2 teaspoons chopped chives
1 teaspoon each of chopped dill,
    thyme and oregano leaves
5 French tarragon leaves
1 garlic clove, finely chopped
3 anchovies
2 teaspoons Cognac or brandy
2 teaspoons Madeira
1 teaspoon Worcestershire sauce
pinch each of sweet paprika, curry
    powder and cayenne
4 white peppercorns
2 teaspoons sea salt
1 tablespoon lemon juice
zest of ½ lemon
zest of ¼ orange
500 g (1 lb 2 oz) unsalted butter

I first moved to Sydney from Melbourne in 1996. It was at the start of my career and I wanted to learn as much as I could about cooking. Luckily, we had some amazing cooking schools in Sydney, and it was at these places that my cooking style started to take shape from watching the best chefs teach their recipes and, more importantly, their philosophies about food. I saw how passionate Neil Perry was about Australian produce, David Thompson did a two-hour class on his love affair with a bowl of rice, and I watched Christine Manfield tea-smoke a duck — the flavours were so new and amazing, and when I tried the duck I was speechless. Back at home I started playing around with flavours; this is the dish I ended up with.

tea-smoked duck breast with foie gras ravioli

SERVES 4

4 x 250 g (9 oz) duck breasts
100 g (3½ oz) foie gras
50 g (1¾ oz) water chestnuts, diced
50 g (1¾ oz) pear, diced
8 gow gee wrappers
250 g (9 oz) baby English spinach
fried crispy ginger, to serve (optional)

ORANGE SAUCE
60 g (2¼ oz) caster (superfine) sugar
3 tablespoons red wine vinegar
500 ml (17 fl oz/2 cups) blood orange juice
250 ml (9 fl oz/1 cup) chicken stock
zest of ¼ orange
50 g (1¾ oz) butter, chopped

TEA-SMOKING MIXTURE
30 g (1 oz/½ cup) oolong tea leaves
30 g (1 oz/½ cup) jasmine tea leaves
zest of 3 oranges
4 pieces of dried orange peel
200 g (7 oz/1 cup) jasmine rice
185 g (6½ oz/1 cup) soft brown sugar
5 star anise
1 tablespoon sichuan peppercorns
6 pieces cassia bark

Line a wok with foil, then place half the smoking mixture on top and turn the heat to medium. Once it starts smoking, place the duck breasts, skin side down, in the middle tray of a steamer or on a rack that fits into the wok and cover with a lid. Cook for 7 minutes or until rare, then remove from heat.

To make the orange sauce, place the sugar in a cold saucepan and melt it down slowly. Add the vinegar and simmer until the sugar is dissolved. Add the orange juice and reduce by half. Add the chicken stock and reduce by half. Add the zest and blend the sauce with the butter and some seasoning.

To make the ravioli, mix the foie gras, water chestnuts and pear with a touch of salt. Lay 4 gow gee wrappers on the bench and brush with water. Place 4 mounds of the foie gras mix in the centre of the gow gees and place the top gow gees over the mounds. Press down firmly around the edges to seal so you have 4 ravioli. Cook the ravioli for 1 minute in a saucepan of boiling water. Drain and set aside.

Preheat a large frying pan to medium–high. Cook the duck, skin side down, until crispy. Turn over and cook for a further minute, then remove and leave to rest for a few minutes. Brush the ravioli with a little oil and cook in the pan until crisp.

Place the spinach into the pan and wilt down with some sea salt and pepper, then drain any excess liquid.

Heat up the orange sauce. Place the spinach on your serving plate, then top with the sliced duck and the ravioli. Drizzle a tablespoon of sauce over the ravioli and duck and top with the fried ginger.

NOTE: This recipes uses half the smoking mixture. It will keep for up to 1 month in an airtight container.

Quite a few recipes I make at home have ended up on my table through eating at friends' restaurants. Since I have had the kids, my days of eating out have decreased drastically. The plus side of that is now I get to spend more time at home doing what I love: cooking.

That said, I do still make time to visit one my of favourite restaurants, Pilu, in Sydney's Freshwater. The owner, Giovanni Pilu, is Sardinian, and his restaurant is one of my all-time favourite places to eat in Australia. It overlooks one of the country's best beaches and he has some of the friendliest staff in town. This is one of his signature dishes and I can't thank him enough for sharing it with me.

porcetto arrosto – giovanni's oven-roasted suckling pig

SERVES 4

Place the suckling pig, skin side up, in a large oiled roasting tin. Cover the skin generously with sea salt and rub in thoroughly, then leave for 15 minutes or until the skin becomes moist. Drizzle oil liberally over the skin and rub in well, then sprinkle with extra sea salt. Preheat the oven to 150°C (300°F/Gas 2).

Roast the pig on the lowest shelf of the oven for 2 hours, or until the skin starts to come away from the top of the meat. Remove from the oven and brush the salt off the skin. Increase the oven to 220°C (425°F/Gas 7). Return the pig to the oven for about 10 minutes or until the skin becomes crisp.

Transfer the pig to a chopping board, cover with foil and leave for 10 minutes, then cut into pieces.

To make the apple sauce, melt the butter in a large frying pan over low heat. Add the apples and cook for about 10 minutes. Add the sugar (if using), cinnamon, cloves and vermouth. Cover and cook, stirring occasionally, until the apples are soft but still chunky.

Serve large chunks of pork with sprigs of rosemary and the apple sauce.

NOTE: You can order suckling pig from speciality butchers.

½ suckling pig, halved lengthways (about 2.5 kg/5 lb 8 oz), head removed (ask your buthcher)
40 g (1½ oz) sea salt
olive oil
rosemary sprigs

APPLE SAUCE
50 g (1¾ oz) butter
6 granny smith apples, peeled, cored and sliced
3 tablespoons caster (superfine) sugar (optional)
a pinch of ground cinnamon
3 cloves, ground
1½ tablespoons vermouth

Wagyu steak comes from a rare breed of cattle that traces its bloodline back to Japan. The amazing thing about this cattle is that it has an increased amount of intermuscular marbling, or fat, than that of regular breeds of cattle. This marbling brings a whole new level of flavour to the meat. This is a luxury item, and I only buy it once or twice a year for special occasions. The rest of the time I just use a nice aged grass-fed piece of meat.

wagyu steak with porcini, kipflers, rocket & shallots

SERVES 4

4 French shallots, peeled
4 x 250 g (9 oz) wagyu sirloin steaks
60 g (2¼ oz) porcini mushrooms or other type of mushroom, sliced
400 g (14 oz) kipfler (fingerling) potatoes, boiled until tender, peeled and sliced
1 garlic clove, peeled and minced
170 ml (5½ fl oz/⅔ cup) veal glacé (see note)
3 tablespoons extra virgin olive oil
1 tablespoon balsamic vinegar
2 large handfuls of wild rocket (arugula)

Preheat the oven to 180°C (350°F/Gas 4). Wrap the shallots in foil and cook in the oven for 30 minutes, or until soft. Set aside to cool slightly, then cut into quarters.

Preheat a grill pan to high. Season each steak with salt and pepper and cook in the greased pan for about 5 minutes, then turn over and cook for a further 4 minutes. Rest for 5 minutes in a warm place.

Meanwhile, place the mushrooms and potatoes on the barbecue hotplate, drizzle with some oil and season with salt and pepper. Cook until golden on both sides, then add the garlic and cook for a further minute. Heat the veal glacé in a small saucepan over medium heat.

Place the potatoes, mushrooms and shallots on serving plates, then slice the meat and place on top. Pour over the veal glacé.

Combine the olive oil and balsamic vinegar. Toss with the rocket and place onto the steak.

NOTE: Veal glacé is a reduction of veal stock available from specialty food stores and some butchers. If unavailable, substitute 250 ml (9 fl oz/1 cup) rich veal or beef stock, reduced by half.

This is one of those special occasion dishes — not to be eaten very often because of the high fat content of the pork belly, but once every so often it really warms the soul. It's traditionally cooked in a clay pot, which is used in a lot of Southeast Asian cookery, but also translates well to the camp oven or a casserole dish with a lid. The saving graces are the water spinach, eggplant and rice because they really balance out the richness of the pork and caramel sauce.

camp oven pork belly with chilli caramel

SERVES 4

Heat the oil in the camp oven over hot coals or a fire to medium–high heat. Add the pork in batches and cook until golden brown. Remove and set aside.

Add the sugar and cook for 1 minute, stirring frequently, or until the sugar dissolves. Add the garlic, ginger, chilli and shallots and cook for 2–3 minutes, or until the sauce turns a deep golden caramel colour.

Add the pork, fish sauce, white pepper, a little salt and 185 ml (6 fl oz/ ¾ cup) of water and mix well. Bring to the boil, then reduce the heat.

Cover and simmer for 1 hour, or until the meat is tender. Add the eggplant and cook for a further 30 minutes. Check the sauce occasionally and add extra water if the sauce becomes too thick or is drying out.

Stir through the water spinach and serve with steamed rice.

1 tablespoon olive or coconut oil
1.5 kg (3 lb 5 oz) pork belly, halved and cut into 3 cm (1¼ inch) thick slices
115 g (4 oz/½ cup) soft brown sugar
4 garlic cloves, peeled and thinly sliced
2 cm (¾ inch) piece ginger, peeled and chopped
1–2 small red chillies, finely chopped
3 red Asian shallots, peeled and thinly sliced
4 tablespoons fish sauce
1 teaspoon ground white pepper
500 g (1 lb 2 oz) Japanese eggplant (aubergine), cut into bite-sized pieces
200 g (7 oz) water spinach or English spinach leaves
steamed jasmine rice, to serve

Cheese on toast is always a big winner, but the occasion should dictate which version of it you make. For entertaining, swap regular bread for a beautiful sourdough and supermarket cheddar for a cheese with lots of flavour and personality, like Gorgonzola. Drizzle over honey that's been flavoured with truffles and you won't believe how quickly these will disappear.

gorgonzola dolce latte with truffled honey & toasted sourdough

SERVES 4

16 thin slices of sourdough
200 g (7 oz) gorgonzola dolce latte or other blue cheese such as roquefort
2 tablespoons truffled honey or other honey
1 bunch of dried or fresh muscatel grapes or fresh figs

Place the cheese on a platter and allow to come to room temperature. Preheat the oven to 180°C (350°F/Gas 4). Put the bread on a baking tray and bake until crisp and light golden.

Heat the honey slightly so that it becomes runny and then drizzle over the cheese. Serve with the bread and fruit.

sweet endings

Ah, dessert. Usually the course people tend to get the most excited for but are too full to eat! I used to make a lot of desserts but now I'm much more likely to be tempted by a fresh piece of fruit than a slice of cake. What can I say, I'm a little older and wiser and not as interested in sugar. But if it's a special occasion or you have the desire for a treat, back in the day these were my favourites. Don't be scared to play around with the ingredients, in fact I urge you to. I would recommend trying stevia as a sugar substitute, or try your hand at baking with coconut flour for a gluten and wheat free option. The granita is a lovely light option and the upside-down plum cake is simple and comforting. Which ever one takes your fancy, remember moderation is the key when choosing to eat dessert, and a small serving is the ideal option when it comes to sweet endings!

Most of the things that bring a smile to my face are simple: surfing, spending time with my kids, fishing, building a campfire in the mountains, snorkelling over a coral reef alive with sea life, listening to someone playing an acoustic guitar and, of course, preparing beautiful meals. The simplest desserts I make are granitas — basically frozen little rocks. I use fruit juice and add sugar syrup and a splash of alcohol that complements the flavour of the juice. Once this is frozen you have the perfect dessert to serve on a hot summer's day or on any day after a big dinner — it refreshes the palate and leaves you feeling cleansed.

Cranberry & Cointreau granita

SERVES 4

To make the sugar syrup, place the sugar and water in a small saucepan over low heat and stir until the sugar dissolves. Increase the heat and bring to the boil. Remove the pan from the heat and set aside to cool.

Mix the cranberry juice, Cointreau, lime juice, orange juice and the 3 tablespoons of sugar syrup together and taste before freezing, adjusting if necessary.

Pour the mixture into a shallow tray and freeze for a few hours. Run a fork through it so it resembles ice shavings.

Meanwhile, to make the cranberry compote, place the cranberries, sugar and cranberry juice in a saucepan and cook until the liquid has reduced and thickened slightly. Allow to cool completely.

Serve the compote with the granita.

SUGAR SYRUP
100 g (3½ oz) caster (superfine) sugar
100 ml (3½ fl oz) water

500 ml (17 fl oz/2 cups) cranberry
   juice
125 ml (4 fl oz/½ cup) Cointreau
25 ml (1 fl oz) strained lime juice
25 ml (1 fl oz) strained fresh orange
   juice
3 tablespoons sugar syrup
   (see above)

CRANBERRY COMPOTE
250 g (9 oz/1⅔ cups) sweetened
   dried cranberries
100 g (3½ oz) caster (superfine) sugar
200 ml (7 fl oz) cranberry juice

Simple and refreshing should be the call for a summer dessert, and what could fit the brief better than this one? It's a bit of a staple at my house — I always have a bottle of champagne in the fridge (for some reason I seem to receive champagne as a gift more often than anything else… obviously I'm not complaining). As far as the gelato or sorbet goes, you can make your own if you have a machine or just go down to the local gelateria or supermarket and buy some. I find the flavours that work best for this are white peach, blood orange, raspberry, strawberry and even lemon.

blood orange sorbet with champagne

SERVES 4

1 litre (35 fl oz/4 cups) freshly
   squeezed blood orange juice
   (or ordinary orange juice), strained
   (about 9 large oranges)
a few mint leaves
500 ml (17 fl oz/2 cups) champagne

STOCK SYRUP
630 g (1 lb 6 oz) caster (superfine)
   sugar
1 cinnamon stick
2 star anise
zest of 1 orange

To make the stock syrup, place all the ingredients in a saucepan with 525 ml (18 fl oz) of water and bring to the boil. Remove from the heat and leave to cool, then strain.

Mix together the stock syrup and orange juice. Churn in an ice-cream machine for 20–30 minutes following the manufacturer's instructions, and then put in the freezer to firm.

Serve scoops of the sorbet with mint leaves and a a good splash of champagne. Serve immediately.

I learned to make zabaglione more than twenty years ago at a place called Mario's in Fitzroy, Melbourne. I couldn't believe how easy and cheap this dessert was to make. This was the dish that taught me all about temperature and the need to be in control of the heat... because the last thing you want to end up with here is a panful of scrambled eggs. The key is to whisk the egg yolks, sugar and alcohol as fast as you can to get as much air into the mixture as possible. The end result should be light and fluffy — it will take about five minutes of whisking, and your arm will probably be pretty sore by the end of it, but it is very rewarding. I love to serve this with macerated berries and sponge finger biscuits to scoop up the zabaglione.

zabaglione with soaked strawberries

SERVES 4

Put the strawberries in a heatproof bowl. Mix the vin santo, honey and sugar in a small pan over medium heat until the sugar dissolves. Pour over the strawberries and leave for 10 minutes, then drain the liquid into another container to use later.

To make the zabaglione, set a stainless steel mixing bowl over a saucepan of barely simmering water. Place the egg yolks, vin santo, balsamic vinegar and sugar in the bowl and whisk for about 5–10 minutes until light and fluffy. Be careful that the water doesn't boil too fast or the eggs will scramble. You can take the bowl off the heat for 10 seconds if it gets too hot (keep whisking!) and then put it back, turning down the heat in the process. (Use a tea towel to hold the bowl — it can get a bit warm.)

Serve the zabaglione with the strawberries and a little of the macerating liquid. I like to use Italian sponge finger biscuits dusted with icing sugar for scooping up the zabaglione.

SOAKED STRAWBERRIES
1 punnet of strawberries, hulled and halved
125 ml (4 fl oz/½ cup) vin santo or other dessert wine
125 ml (4 fl oz/½ cup) honey
3 tablespoons caster (superfine) sugar

ZABAGLIONE
8 free-range egg yolks
170 ml (5½ fl oz/⅔ cup) vin santo or other dessert wine
1 tablespoon aged balsamic vinegar
230 g (8 oz/⅓ cup) caster (superfine) sugar

Italian sponge finger biscuits
icing (confectioners') sugar, for dusting

This is one recipe that is super easy to make and always stands out as the crowd favourite. You can team it with just about any fruit in season. I know goat's curd doesn't sound like a great cheese to put into a dessert but, trust me, this is an absolute winner.

goat's curd cheesecake with passionfruit sauce

SERVES 4

BASE
140 g (5 oz) almonds, roasted and
    cooled
2 teaspoons white sesame seeds
70 g (2½ oz) unsalted butter

400 ml (14 fl oz) thickened cream
300 g (10½ oz) goat's curd
150 g (5½ oz) caster (superfine) sugar
zest and juice of 1 lemon
3 gelatine leaves or 3 teaspoons
    powdered gelatine

PASSIONFRUIT SAUCE
250 g (9 oz) passionfruit pulp
125 g (4½ oz) caster (superfine) sugar

To make the base, blend the almonds and sesame seeds in a food processor. Melt the butter in a frying pan until it turns brown, then pour just enough into the nut mixture to combine.

Grease a 20 cm (8 inch) springform cake tin. Line the base and side with baking paper, then lightly grease. Press the base mixture into the tin and leave to set in the fridge.

Gently heat the cream, goat's curd, sugar and lemon in a pan. Soak the gelatine leaves in 250 ml (9 fl oz/1 cup) cold water for 2 minutes, then squeeze out the water. Whisk into the pan of cream, then strain it all into a bowl. If using powdered gelatine, stir it into 3 tablespoons of boiling water, leave to sit for 1 minute, then add to the cream.

Pour the cream filling into the tin and leave to set for 4–5 hours in the fridge.

To make the passionfruit sauce, blend the pulp, then strain to separate the juice. Measure the juice and then add an equal amount of water. Put the sugar in a saucepan with 1 cm (½ inch) of water over medium–high heat and boil until caramel. Add the juice and water mixture and cook until syrupy, then add the passionfruit seeds. Leave to cool slightly. Cut the cheesecake with a hot knife and serve with the sauce.

You've got to love a good apple dessert, and this one takes the cake. It looks great and will have your family and guests loving your originality. Instead of having to cook individual soufflés, which can be a bit hard to get consistent in some ovens, this is a cheat's way to achieve the beautiful lightness and finesse of a soufflé without the difficulty. You can play around with whatever fruit is in season, but in the winter months it's hard to go past cooked apple and pears spiced with cinnamon.

pear, apple & cinnamon pan soufflé

SERVES 4–6

To make the cinnamon caramel, combine all the ingredients in a small saucepan, then stir until the sugar dissolves and the butter melts. Bring to the boil and simmer, uncovered, until thickened slightly; keep warm.

Peel and core the apples and cut into eighths. Repeat with the pears without peeling them.

Put the butter in a 25 cm (10 inch) non-stick ovenproof frying pan over medium heat. Once the butter has melted, add the fruit and pan-fry until golden and starting to soften. Add half of the sugar and cook until caramelised.

In a large bowl, whisk the egg yolks with the lemon rind, honey, rum and cinnamon. Beat the egg whites and remaining sugar in a clean bowl using an electric mixer until soft peaks form.

Fold the egg white mixture into the egg yolk mixture and pour over the fruit in the frying pan. Shake the pan slightly to allow the mixture to settle around the fruit. Cook over medium heat until the mixture starts to set.

Meanwhile, preheat the grill (broiler) to very hot. Place the pan under the grill and cook until lightly browned on the top. Top with the mascarpone and cinnamon caramel.

CINNAMON CARAMEL
110 g (3¾ oz/½ cup) firmly packed
   soft brown sugar
30 g (1 oz) unsalted butter, softened
1 tablespoon water
½ teaspoon ground cinnamon

2 granny smith apples
2 large firm beurre bosc pears
50 g (1¾ oz) unsalted butter,
   chopped
3 tablespoons soft brown sugar
4 free-range eggs, separated
1 teaspoon finely grated lemon rind
1 tablespoon organic honey
2 tablespoons rum
½ teaspoon ground cinnamon
250 g (9 oz) mascarpone cheese

The easiest and most beautiful dessert in the world is panna cotta, which basically means cream that has been set. It was the first dessert I learned to make as an apprentice and I used to love making it because I knew it was very hard to get it wrong, which meant that I didn't get in trouble from the head chef. I have served these yoghurt panna cottas with blueberries as I love the flavour of lightly warmed and infused blueberries, but feel free to try them with any fruit you like.

yoghurt panna cotta with blueberries

SERVES 8

375 ml (13 fl oz/1½ cups) thickened cream
1 vanilla bean, split in half lengthways and seeds scraped out
115 g (4 oz/½ cup) caster (superfine) sugar
2 teaspoons powdered gelatine
560 g (1 lb 4 oz/2¼ cups) plain yoghurt

BLUEBERRY SAUCE
220 g (7¾ oz/1 cup) caster (superfine) sugar
3 tablespoons sparkling or white wine
1 vanilla bean, split in half lengthways and seeds scraped out
1 cinnamon stick
1 star anise
375 g (13 oz) frozen blueberries
1–2 tablespoons lemon juice

Combine half the cream with the vanilla bean, vanilla seeds and sugar in a saucepan. Bring slowly to the boil, stirring constantly, until the sugar dissolves.

Sprinkle the gelatine over 2 tablespoons of water in a heatproof cup or jug. Place the cup of gelatine mixture in a small saucepan of gently simmering water, without letting the water spill into the cup. Alternatively, microwave it on high (100%) for about 20 seconds, until dissolved.

Stir the gelatine into the cream mixture. (If using leaf gelatine, soften in cold water for 5 minutes, squeeze out the excess water, then add to the cream mixture and stir until dissolved.) Pour the hot cream mixture into a heatproof bowl. Remove the vanilla bean and cool to room temperature. Gradually stir the yoghurt into the cooled cream mixture.

Beat the remaining cream in a small bowl using an electric mixer until soft peaks form. Gently fold the whipped cream into the yoghurt mixture. Spoon the mixture into eight lightly oiled 125 ml (4 fl oz/½ cup) capacity glasses or moulds; cover and refrigerate for 4 hours or overnight.

Meanwhile, to make the blueberry sauce, combine the sugar with 125 ml (4 fl oz/½ cup) of water in a small saucepan and stir over low heat, without boiling, until the sugar dissolves. Bring to the boil; boil, uncovered for about 8 minutes or until honey-coloured. Carefully add the wine, vanilla bean and seeds, cinnamon, star anise and blueberries; cook gently for 2 minutes. Remove from the heat. Add the lemon juice to taste; cool to room temperature. Remove the spices.

Serve the panna cottas with the blueberry sauce.

NOTE: If you want to turn out the panna cotta, make the mixture a little firmer by using 3 teaspoons of gelatine.

If you have a sweet tooth, this dessert is going to satisfy it on so many levels. Although the cake is delicious on its own, I think a few drizzles of warm butterscotch sauce and the red wine strawberries take it to a whole other level. It is a really decadent way to finish off a good meal, and a little goes a long way.

chocolate & sticky date pudding with butterscotch sauce & red wine strawberries

SERVES 8–10

To make the butterscotch sauce, combine the brown sugar, butter and cream in a pan over medium heat. Bring to the boil, stirring, then simmer for 5 minutes.

Line a 25 cm (10 inch) springform cake tin with greased baking paper. Pour in half of the butterscotch sauce (keep the rest for serving).

Mix the dates and bicarbonate of soda in a small bowl. Pour in 600 ml (21 fl oz) of boiling water and leave to cool. Preheat the oven to 180°C (350°F/Gas 4).

Beat the sugar, butter and vanilla seeds in a bowl until creamy. Add in the eggs and beat well. Mix in the date mixture. Sift together the flour and baking powder and add to the bowl. Stir in the chocolate.

Pour into the tin and bake for 30 minutes, then reduce the heat to 160°C (315°F/Gas 2–3) and cook for another hour. Test with a skewer, then remove from the oven and cool in the tin before turning out.

Meanwhile, to make the red wine strawberries, mix the sugar with 3 tablespoons of water in a pan to form a paste. Heat until it turns light caramel, then add the red wine (be careful; it will spit) and stir. Add the cinnamon and cook for 10 minutes. Pour over the strawberries and leave to macerate for up to an hour before serving.

Cut the pudding into slices and pour the butterscotch sauce over the top. If necessary, heat the sauce in the microwave until warm and serve with cream and red wine strawberries.

BUTTERSCOTCH SAUCE
300 g (10½ oz) soft brown sugar
150 g (5½ oz) unsalted butter
150 ml (5 fl oz) cream

300 g (10½ oz) pitted dates, cut in half
2 teaspoons bicarbonate of soda
200 g (7 oz) soft brown sugar
120 g (4 oz) unsalted butter
1 vanilla bean, split in half lengthways and seeds scraped out
2 free-range eggs
460 g (1 lb) plain (all-purpose) flour
3 teaspoons baking powder
300 g (10½ oz) chocolate buttons
thick cream, to serve

RED WINE STRAWBERRIES
115 g (4 oz/½ cup) caster (superfine) sugar
250 ml (9 fl oz/1 cup) pinot noir
1 cinnamon stick
1 punnet of strawberries, hulled and halved

Baking has really exploded in popularity in recent years and every time I turn around there's a new craze: cupcakes, macaroons, whoopee pies ... the creativity is incredible. And I'm all for that because it makes life exciting. That said, I believe there's still something very special about the simpler cakes a lot of us grew up with. And that's what this cake is all about: a few beautiful flavours, seasonal stone fruit and not much fuss. I'll take a slice of this over a fancy cake any day.

upside-down plum cake

SERVES 8–10

1 tablespoon soft brown sugar
6 large plums, halved, stones removed
225 g (8 oz) unsalted butter, softened
170 g (5¾ oz/¾ cup) caster (superfine) sugar
extra 115 g (4 oz/½ cup firmly packed) soft brown sugar
1 teaspoon vanilla extract
3 free-range eggs
150 g (5½ oz/1 cup) plain (all-purpose) flour
110 g (3¾ oz/¾ cup) self-raising flour
¾ teaspoon bicarbonate of soda (baking soda)
1 teaspoon ground cinnamon
45 g (1½ oz/½ cup) flaked almonds
2 tablespoons milk
whipped cream, to serve

Preheat the oven to 140°C (275°F/Gas 1). Grease a deep 22 cm (8½ inch) round cake tin and line the base with baking paper.

Sprinkle the 1 tablespoon of brown sugar over the base of the tin, then arrange the plums, cut side down, on top of the sugar.

Using an electric mixer beat the butter, caster sugar, extra brown sugar and vanilla extract in a bowl until light and fluffy. Add the eggs, then sift in the combined flours, bicarbonate of soda and cinnamon. Beat gently until combined. Add the almonds and milk, then mix until just combined. Spoon the mixture into the prepared tin and spread evenly over the plums.

Bake for 1 hour 20 minutes, or until cooked when tested with a skewer. Stand the cake in the tin for 15 minutes before turning onto a serving plate. Serve warm, accompanied by whipped cream, or cool to room temperature and serve cold.

A few years ago I was lucky enough to work with a unique culinary talent — Sammie Coryton. She has a wonderfully playful relationship with food preparation that I'm in awe of. This pie is one of my favourite recipes of hers. If you love desserts that are full of flavour and have everyone wanting more, then this is it. I've served this pie to many friends in my own home and it always gets a very enthusiastic reaction. Sammie is now the owner of a majestic castle in the English countryside called Pentillie Estate and she caters for weddings with her scrumptious food. If you are getting hitched and want to ensure the food is top-notch, make sure you look her up.

open cherry pie

SERVES 8

Combine the flour, icing sugar mixture and a pinch of salt in a food processor and process briefly until combined. Add the butter, cream cheese and vanilla. Process until the mixture is just combined and resembles very coarse breadcrumbs. Add about 1½ tablespoons of water and process until the mixture just comes together. If you need to add more water, add a few drops at a time. Tip onto a lightly floured workbench and knead briefly until smooth (the dough will be quite soft). Shape into a flat disc and wrap in plastic wrap; refrigerate for 1 hour. Meanwhile, preheat the oven to 220°C (425°F/Gas 7) and lightly grease a large baking tray.

Make the cherry filling just before needed. Put all the ingredients in a large bowl and stir to combine.

Roll the pastry out to a circle about 40–45 cm (16–17¾ inches) in diameter; do not trim. Carefully lift the pastry onto the baking tray. Pile the filling into the centre of the pastry (in a mound about 20 cm/8 inches in diameter) and bring the pastry edges up over the top of the cherries, leaving an opening. Brush the exposed pastry with a little milk, then sprinkle with sugar. Bake for 20 minutes, then reduce the temperature to 190°C (375°F/Gas 5) and bake for a further 30 minutes, or until the pastry is golden. Cover the pie with foil if it's browning too quickly.

Serve the pie with vanilla bean ice cream or cream, if you like.

250 g (9 oz/1⅔ cups) plain (all-purpose) flour
2 tablespoons icing (confectioners') sugar mixture
pinch of salt
100 g (3½ oz) chilled unsalted butter, chopped
100 g (3½ oz) chilled cream cheese, chopped
½ teaspoon vanilla bean paste
milk, to brush
2 tablespoons caster (superfine) sugar

CHERRY FILLING

800 g (1 lb 12 oz) cherries, pitted (about 600 g/1 lb 5 oz pitted weight)
115 g (4 oz/½ cup) caster (superfine) sugar
3 tablespoons finely grated dark chocolate
½ teaspoon mixed spice
½ teaspoon vanilla bean paste
1 tablespoon lemon juice
2 tablespoons arrowroot or cornflour (cornstarch)

These would have to be the most indulgent and addictive dessert on the face of the planet. They are so good they should probably have a government health warning. The funny thing is that in Spain these are actually eaten for breakfast, in the same way that the French eat *pain au chocolate* (something else I can't get my head around). These are easy to make — just make sure the oil for deep-frying is fresh and you haven't cooked spring rolls or salt and pepper squid in there, otherwise you'll get some pretty strange flavours lurking in your doughnuts. Traditionally these are dusted with plain sugar but I also like to add a little cinnamon. Enjoy.

churros with hot chocolate sauce

MAKES ABOUT 25–30 CHURROS

CHOCOLATE SAUCE
200 ml (7 fl oz) cream
200 g (7 oz) dark chocolate, roughly chopped

CINNAMON SUGAR
55 g (2 oz/¼ cup) caster (superfine) sugar
1 teaspoon ground cinnamon
coconut or olive oil, for deep-frying
2 tablespoons soft brown sugar
½ teaspoon salt
70 g (2½ oz/⅓ cup) unsalted butter, softened
125 g (4½ oz/1 cup) plain (all-purpose) flour
2 free-range eggs
½ teaspoon vanilla extract

To make the chocolate sauce, heat the cream in a saucepan over medium heat until hot. Put the chocolate in a bowl, pour in the hot cream and mix until smooth. Keep warm until needed.

To make the cinnamon sugar, mix the sugar and cinnamon together and set aside.

Fill a large deep frying pan one-third full of oil and heat to 180°C (350°F). Be sure to keep your eye on the pan at all times.

Combine the brown sugar, salt, butter and 250 ml (9 fl oz/1 cup) of water in a saucepan over medium heat. Bring to the boil, then remove from the heat and stir in the flour. Whisk together the eggs and vanilla, add to the pan and stir well.

Attach a large star nozzle to your piping bag and fill the bag with the churros dough.

Test your oil by squeezing a small amount of dough into it. The dough should bubble up right away. If it doesn't, the oil is not hot enough.

Once the oil is hot, squeeze 10 cm (4 inch) lengths of dough into the oil. You should be able to cook four or five churros at a time. Cook for about 2 minutes, then turn with a slotted spoon. Cook for another 2–3 minutes until golden brown. Remove with a slotted spoon and drain on kitchen paper.

While still warm, roll the churros in the cinnamon sugar, then serve with hot chocolate sauce.

This is the first dessert pizza I ever created. I wanted something on the menu that customers couldn't resist. It had to have chocolate, hazelnuts, bananas, honey and ice cream or gelato. I think this is one of the best pizzas I've ever created, and it's fantastically easy to make at home. Buy the best-quality ice cream or gelato you can to top this special dessert pizza.

chocolate, hazelnut & banana pizza with vanilla gelato

MAKES ONE 15 X 10 CM (6 X 4 INCH) OVAL PIZZA / SERVES 2–4

Place a pizza stone in the oven and preheat the oven to 250°C (500°F/ Gas 9) or to its highest temperature. Once it has reached the temperature, it will take about 15 minutes for the pizza stone to heat up.

Lightly dust a clean work surface with semolina or flour, and then roll out the dough ball into a 15 x 10 cm (6 x 4 inch) oval that is about 3 mm (1/8 inch) thick. Transfer the pizza base onto a piece of baking paper; this is necessary for transferring the assembled pizza to the pizza stone. Prick the pizza base all over with a fork or docker.

Spread the chocolate-hazelnut paste evenly over the pizza base. Place the sliced banana neatly on top, then the ricotta cheese.

Transfer the pizza onto the heated pizza stone and cook the pizza for 5–10 minutes or until golden and crisp. Shave the chocolate, at room temperature, with a knife. Refrigerate to prevent the shavings from melting when serving.

Using a pizza paddle or wide spatula, carefully transfer the pizza to a chopping board or plate. Dollop on a scoop of ice cream and sprinkle over the chocolate shavings and hazelnuts. Drizzle over the honey and dust with icing sugar, if desired, before serving.

semolina or plain (all-purpose) flour, for dusting

120 g (4¼ oz) pizza dough ball (see pages 212–213)

3 tablespoons chocolate-hazelnut paste

1 banana, sliced and coated in lemon juice

1 tablespoon fresh ricotta cheese, broken into pieces

1 scoop vanilla ice cream or gelato, to serve

2 tablespoons chocolate, shaved

2 tablespoons hazelnuts, toasted, peeled and chopped

2 teaspoons honey

icing (confectioners') sugar, for dusting (optional)

The following is a really simple dessert idea for your barbecue. Always make sure, that you clean your barbecue thoroughly before attempting to grill your fruit as you don't want any residual flavours from your steak marinade or barbecued squid to ruin the delicious ripe fruit.

barbecued peaches with amaretto

SERVES 4

460 g (1 lb/2 cups) caster (superfine) sugar
2 x 5 cm (2 inch) pieces orange zest
125 ml (4 fl oz/½ cup) fresh orange juice
125 ml (4 fl oz/½ cup) amaretto liqueur (Galliano brand works well)
1 vanilla pod, split in half lengthways and seeds scraped out
6 firm peaches, halved and stones removed
80 g (2¾ oz/½ cup) almonds, toasted and roughly chopped

ALMOND AMARETTO CREAM
300 ml (10½ fl oz) thickened (whipping) cream
3 tablespoons icing (confectioners') sugar
250 g (9 oz) mascarpone cheese
2 tablespoons amaretto liqueur
100 g (3½ oz) amaretti biscuits, coarsely chopped

To make the almond amaretto cream, beat the cream with 1 tablespoon icing sugar until soft peaks form. Stir the mascarpone with the remaining icing sugar, amaretto and biscuits until just combined. Gently fold the whipped cream into the mascarpone mixture until just combined. Refrigerate for at least 4 hours before serving.

Place the sugar, zest, orange juice, amaretto, vanilla and 250 ml (9 fl oz/1 cup) of water in a large saucepan. Stir over a low heat until the sugar dissolves. Bring to the boil and then remove from the heat and cool until warm. Pour over the peaches in a large baking dish. Set aside to cool.

Preheat barbecue hotplate or grill to medium–high. Remove the peaches from the syrup, reserving the syrup. Cook the peaches on oiled hotplate or grill for 5 minutes or until golden brown.

Place the peaches on a platter and pour some of the syrup over the top. Garnish with toasted almonds and serve with almond amaretto cream on the side.

I guess I would call this a peasant dish. Peasant dishes are often the yummiest because it's a recipe using a few basic ingredients cooked with love and passed down from generation to generation. Rice pudding is a dessert that reminds me of childhood — here I have teamed it with rhubarb as I love the flavour and colour after slow cooking it with spices.

rice pudding with red wine poached rhubarb

Preheat the oven to 160°C (315°F/Gas 2–3). Combine the milk, cream, sugar, bay leaf, lemon rind, pepper and vanilla in a saucepan. Bring to the boil, stirring to dissolve the sugar. Add the rice, stir well and remove from the heat.

Tip the rice mixture into a 2 litre (8 cup) capacity baking dish, then cover with foil. Bake for about 1 hour, stirring occasionally, until the rice is tender and most of the liquid has been absorbed. The rice will absorb any extra liquid on standing, so don't panic unless it's swimming in milk. If this is the case, bake for a further 10 minutes.

Meanwhile, to make the poached rhubarb, bring the wine, sugar and 125 ml (4 fl oz/½ cup) of water to the boil; simmer, uncovered, for 10 minutes. Add the rhubarb and return to the boil. Remove immediately from the heat and stand until cold. Carefully remove the cooked rhubarb from the poaching juices using a slotted spoon. Bring the poaching liquid back to the boil and simmer, uncovered, until reduced by two-thirds.

Serve the rice pudding with the poached rhubarb and drizzle with some of the poaching liquid.

500 ml (17 fl oz/2 cups) milk
500 ml (17 fl oz/2 cups) cream
80 g (2¾ oz/⅓ cup) caster (superfine) sugar
1 dried bay leaf
2 long strips of lemon rind, removed with a vegetable peeler
¼ teaspoon ground black pepper
1 teaspoon vanilla extract or 1 vanilla bean, split in half lengthways and seeds scraped out
120 g (4¼ oz/½ cup) white medium-grain rice

POACHED RHUBARB
250 ml (9 fl oz/1 cup) red wine (such as shiraz)
230 g (8 oz/1 cup) caster (superfine) sugar
400 g (14 oz) rhubarb, trimmed, cut into 6 cm (2½ inch) lengths

index